Advance Praise for

EXIT WITHOUT LEAVING

"I used to think if I just worked harder and hired good people, the rest would take care of itself. Then I read *Exit Without Leaving* and realized I'd built a strong business that still depended too much on me. Harrison doesn't just talk about leadership. He holds a mirror up to it. Through stories, humor, and uncomfortable truths, he lays out a framework that's both simple and challenging. We've started asking better questions, empowering our leaders to be the door— not the ceiling—and I'm seeing more clarity, accountability, and energy across the board. It's not magic, but it's close."

—**LARRY WEIGAND**, CEO of
Weigand Construction Incorporated

"Harrison's an artist in his organizational leadership and illustrations. Anyone who wants a stronger business should read this book."

—**NICK DANCER**, President of DANCER

"*Exit Without Leaving* gave us language and clarity around what really matters. We stopped chasing every opportunity and started building strategically—from people to systems to customers. It's been a game-changer for sustainable growth."

—**NEIL RYAN**, President of Mt. Carmel Stabilization Group, Inc.

"Succession planning usually sounds like a dry business school topic, but Harrison Tash makes it real, relevant, and honestly, kind of urgent. *Exit Without Leaving* is about more than just transitions. It's about leaving something stronger than you found it. As a leader who thinks a lot about legacy, storytelling, and building something bigger than yourself, this book really hit home. Harrison gets it, and he helps the rest of us get it too."

—KEN KLUG, CEO, QCS Purchasing Cooperative

"Our company was growing and thriving with an inevitable growth plateau approaching—employee burnout, market or technology changes, or something else. *Exit Without Leaving* helped us focus on the vital steps necessary for the near and long-term future growth of our business with a focus on people and culture as the economic engine and energy needed to drive us forward. The ideas presented are easy to understand and organized into actionable steps for implementation."

—TONY TRANQUILL, CEO and
President of Wayne Pipe & Supply

"What impressed me most about *Exit Without Leaving* is how it ties the intangible (like culture) to the measurable (like revenue growth). The 8 to Great framework elevates both people and performance without compromising either."

—NICHOLAS RIVECCA, President of Riv/Crete Readymix

"*Exit Without Leaving* doesn't just tell you how to lead better. It shows you how to build something that lasts, with practical, proven tactics. If you're serious about leveling up as a leader and growing a healthier, more sustainable organization, this book is for you."

—ANDREW GRITZMAKER, CEO and President
of YMCA of Greater Fort Wayne

"We were 'successful' on paper, but burning out behind the scenes. *Exit Without Leaving* helped us stop grinding and start growing—with intention. Turns out, when your people are healthy and your systems aren't duct-taped together, magic happens."

—MATT METZGER, Vice President, Property Tax, DMA Inc

EXIT
WITHOUT
LEAVING

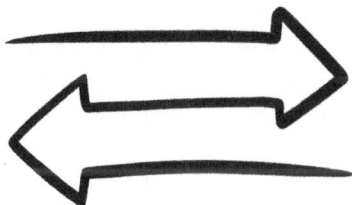

**Building a Business That Thrives with
You but Doesn't Depend on You**

HARRISON TASH

A

AUTHOR.INC

EXIT WITHOUT LEAVING
Building a Business That Thrives with You but Doesn't Depend on You
First Edition

Edited by Lisa Caskey, David Caissie, and Cypriene Madison
Cover design by Pete Garceau
Interior design by John van der Woude, JVDW Designs

ISBN   978-1-966372-05-9   *Hardcover*
       978-1-966372-04-2   *Paperback*
       978-1-966372-03-5   *eBook*

Published by Author.Inc

This book is intended to provide general information on the subject matter covered. It is provided with the understanding that the author and publisher are not rendering legal, financial, medical, psychological, or other professional advice. Readers should consult licensed professionals for advice relevant to their situation.

To get the full value of joy, you must have someone to divide it with.
—MARK TWAIN

To my wife, Ash, and kids, Alexis and Levi, we're always "Better Together."

To my parents, Jason and Patricia— thank you for always encouraging and supporting my entrepreneurial journey.

CONTENTS

STARTING
POINT

"I've told you a thousand times how to do it. Why can't you just get it right?!"

The owner's voice cut through the room, sharp and frustrated. The tension was thick, made worse by the dull hum of fluorescent lights overhead. Working for this business wasn't quite the experience I had imagined. Fresh out of college, I was getting a crash course in what it really meant to be part of a small business: the backbone of the economy, yet often chaotic and overwhelmed.

This company had an idea for its future, but no clear path to get there. They weren't bad people. Rather, they were just stuck, frustrated by employees who weren't on the same page, struggling to create consistency, and uncertain how to develop their team. They were great at *the work* but never signed up for the headaches that came with growth. Yet, demand kept coming. Customers wanted what they had to offer, so the growing pains continued.

SUFFERING WHILE GROWING YOUR BUSINESS?

If you've felt the challenge of scaling a business while navigating the pain that comes with it, you're not alone. There are 3 major struggles that you might identify with when growing your business:

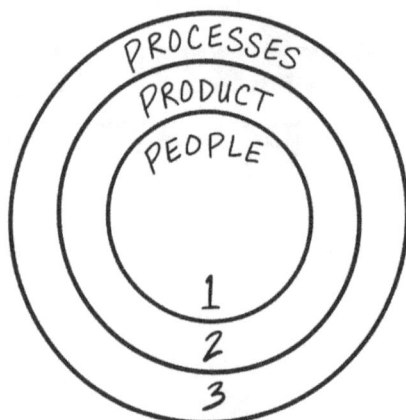

1. People

Maybe it's your people (or, maybe it's you) who can't keep up. Have you thought or said things like this?

> *"I feel like I'm running in circles trying to get things done."*
> *"I'm tired of keeping others on track."*
> *"I want to be a better leader, but I'm not even sure where to start. I'm just trying to keep up with what's in front of me."*

2. Product

It might be your quality. Possibly your product or service has suffered in recent years. Maybe you've said or thought things like this:

"They don't do it like I do. It's just easier to do it myself."

"I can't sit next to them all day, ensuring they get it done the way it should be done."

"I don't want to make more money at the expense of losing our quality."

3. Processes

Or maybe it's your processes. You don't have a great system to help keep things moving, aligned, and heading in the right direction. You might have said or thought something like this:

"Why do we do it differently every time? We don't need to reinvent the wheel."

"They do whatever they want, and I'm tired of it affecting our company."

You don't need a lifetime to build a self-sustaining business— one that thrives with you but doesn't depend on you. Freedom comes when you invest in people, lead with purpose, and streamline your operations.

THE DREAM: A COMPANY THAT OPERATES ON ITS OWN

Maybe you feel that you're a lifetime away from a company that operates on its own. You might have seen other companies over the years that seemed to run so smoothly, your jaw dropped thinking, *How do they run like a well-oiled machine? Where the heck did they find those people? What's their secret sauce?* Maybe you think you could never get there, or maybe you tried, but it felt like you were pushing a boulder up a hill. At some point, you've possibly had those moments that seemed like you did get there, then within that same week, you were dragging your hands down your face in stress.

Since you've picked up this book, you've likely been just like me at one point. You want to get off the chaos roller coaster. You've figured out how to make some money. You've spent the long nights working on the next project or stayed up late worrying about how to pay employees on Friday. Now, years later, you have confidence that you can keep the lights on, but you want to create a better version of your business. You want a business where you're in control.

You've probably created the ideal business in your head. Maybe for you, it's having a great team that runs the company. Maybe it's having an amazing service or product so dialed in that customers don't call anyone else. Maybe you want to be more efficient, run like clockwork. Most likely, you want *all* of that. It all sounds good, and it's not out of reach.

But here's the truth: you won't find any *get-rich-quick* gimmicks in this book. There are no major shortcuts, and no overnight success formula. Real success takes intention and time.

AIM HIGHER, BUILD SMARTER

My clients typically have built their businesses off hard work and grit. Most have anywhere from ten to hundreds of employees. They started doing what they loved or what was in demand, and before they knew it, they were making millions in revenue.

If you're like them, you found yourself saying, "There has to be a better way this time around." You're done pushing as fast as you can and seeing what sticks. This next chapter of your business, you want better. I wouldn't put this book in front of you without first testing and refining it through true application with many businesses like yours.

This book is different from what you've read before: I have clearly illustrated (I literally sketched drawings) in simple ways that help you apply the framework faster. By reading this book, you will change the way you think about your business. You'll have a standard to take your business to the next level and a practical way of implementing it today.

There's only 1 thing I ask as you read further: I need you to believe you can become that business you've always dreamed of. It *is* possible, but you must believe it can happen. This is called the *Pygmalion effect*. (That's pig-male-e-on, if you need a handicap like me.) It's a psychological phenomenon that describes how expectations can impact performance. It's based on the idea that people tend to work harder to meet high expectations. Doing the same thing that you've done for the last 10 years is not going to get you the results you want for the next 10.

The businesses that I've helped are not smarter or work harder than you. They have simply raised their expectations to new heights. They have implemented the 8 to Great framework and consistently chose to stick with it. Their outcomes have compounded over time because they raised their expectations and believed it was possible.

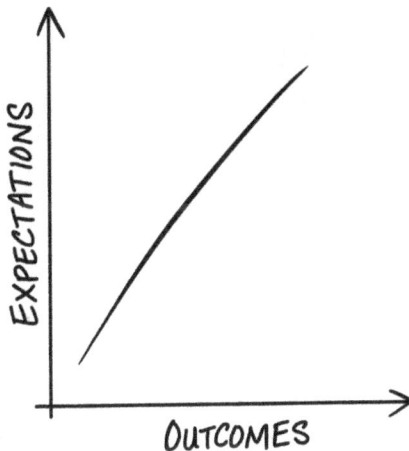

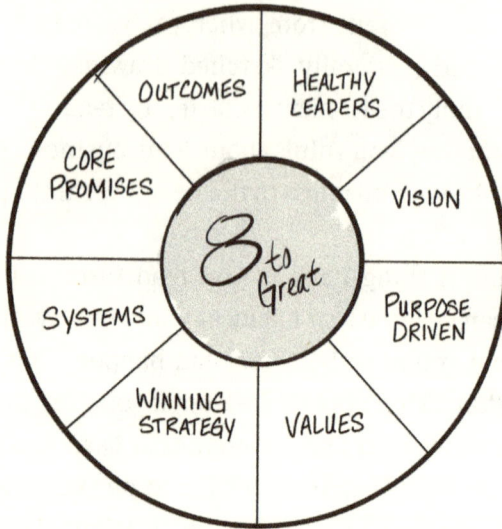

8 TO GREAT

The 8 to Great framework is holistic, forged from observations and refined by real businesses just like yours through our consulting work. I have collected timeless principles and worked through real-life applications of how each component fuels a self-sustaining business and gives you a unique edge. Let's break the model down a bit.

The first 4 components are:

1. Healthy Leaders
2. Vision
3. Purpose Driven
4. Values

I call these the Foundational 4, because the second 4 are unsustainable if these are not integrated into the fabric of your business. To integrate the Foundational 4 well, you must first believe your company is a living, breathing organism. It needs to be nourished daily. Starving the business of these will inevitably choke the rest of your company.

The second set is the Operational 4:

1. Winning Strategy
2. Systems
3. Core Promises
4. Outcomes

The Operational 4 are strengthened by the Foundational 4. Life is given to the operation based on the strength of the foundation.

Let me give this some meat right away to help you with why this matters: we should all understand that it isn't only about the *who*, but also the *how*. It's as much about the people as it is the process. This tricky balance is what we've all struggled with at some point in our businesses.

CULTURE HAPPENS WHETHER YOU MEAN IT TO OR NOT

We're not just talking about your company; we're talking about something deeper. The companies that we wish to emulate likely also have something that's hard to put your finger on. Sometimes, we call this culture.

There's a vital part of the 8 to Great that can be easy to overlook—culture. Though it's not 1 of the 8 components, culture is the by-product of *how and why* you integrate them into your business. Culture is not hard to see but can be hard to define. Without a culture that attracts people, you're just another company in a sea of competitors. The sharks are real, and if you're not careful, the big sharks will take you out.

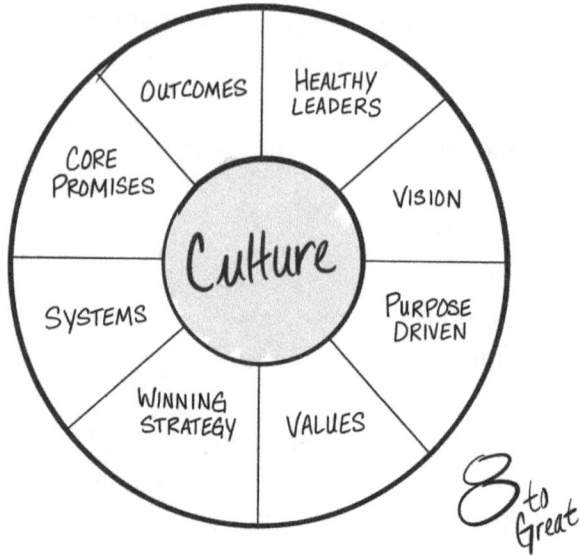

Good news though: thriving companies have something that sets them apart—they're different. They're not competing for the bottom feeders; they have a culture that people love and customers want more of. Throughout this book, I'll share key ways to make a lasting, thriving culture. Not a *beanbag-chair-in-the-break-room* type of culture, but one that is fueled on performance, likes to create and *do*, and where people share a vision and enjoy working next to each other. Culture is the invisible force that either supercharges your growth or quietly pulls you under.

You'll notice Mark Twain quotes sprinkled throughout this book. That's no accident. Twain's humor, wisdom, and unapologetic clarity have shaped more than just my thinking; they've helped shape our company's values. His words have a way of cutting through the noise and naming what most people are too polite (or too buttoned-up) to say out loud.

I've leaned on Twain's wit over the years to keep things light when the work gets heavy, and to remind myself (and my clients) that clear thinking doesn't have to be complicated. Sometimes, the right quote at the right moment can snap a team out of the weeds faster than a dozen bullet points. So, if you find yourself chuckling or thinking, *Dang, that hits*, you're in good company. Twain's along for the ride, and I'm glad you are too.

IF YOU THINK THIS WON'T WORK FOR YOU, READ THIS FIRST

I know what you're thinking: *These are the simple things that I've tried in the past. They don't work.* This is what I call *Envy Downplay.* It's way easier to think that it won't work for you because others have something that you don't. You downplay your envy and disregard it, thinking, *That works for others but not me.*

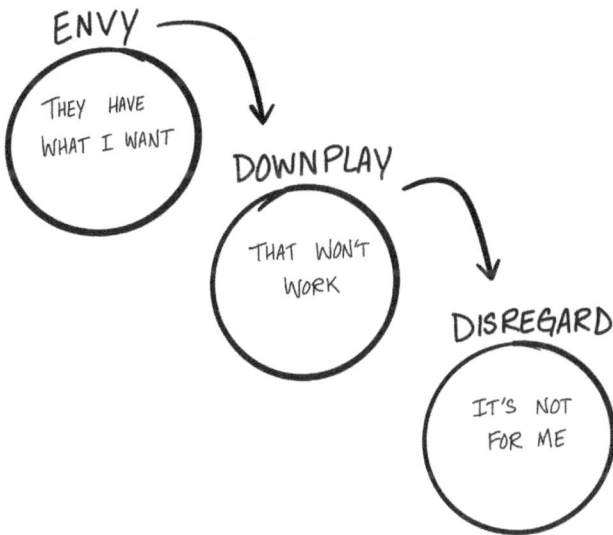

ENVY

THEY HAVE
WHAT I WANT

DOWNPLAY

THAT WON'T
WORK

DISREGARD

IT'S NOT
FOR ME

Or maybe your hang-up is the *too simple complex.* Maybe you think, *There's no way on God's green Earth that this is the answer. It's just too simple and easy.*

You're right; it's not easy. That's exactly why I wrote this book. If you're feeling skeptical, I understand. There are countless books that offer a single tactic or narrow solution. But this one's different. It takes a more holistic approach, connecting the dots across all the key areas and showing you a clear, integrated path forward.

This book was written for business leaders who want a company that thrives with them but doesn't depend on them. This is for people who aren't just chasing another buck—they're building something impactful and lasting.

This is for the leaders who understand that success isn't a finish line; it's a journey. Whether you're at the top of your game or still climbing, this book will help you uncover the tools, strategies, and mindset to not only sustain success, but to elevate your business beyond what you thought possible.

No matter where you are, if you're ready to lead with purpose, align your people, and build a self-sustaining thriving business, then keep reading because the best is yet to come.

PART 1

FOUNDATIONAL 4

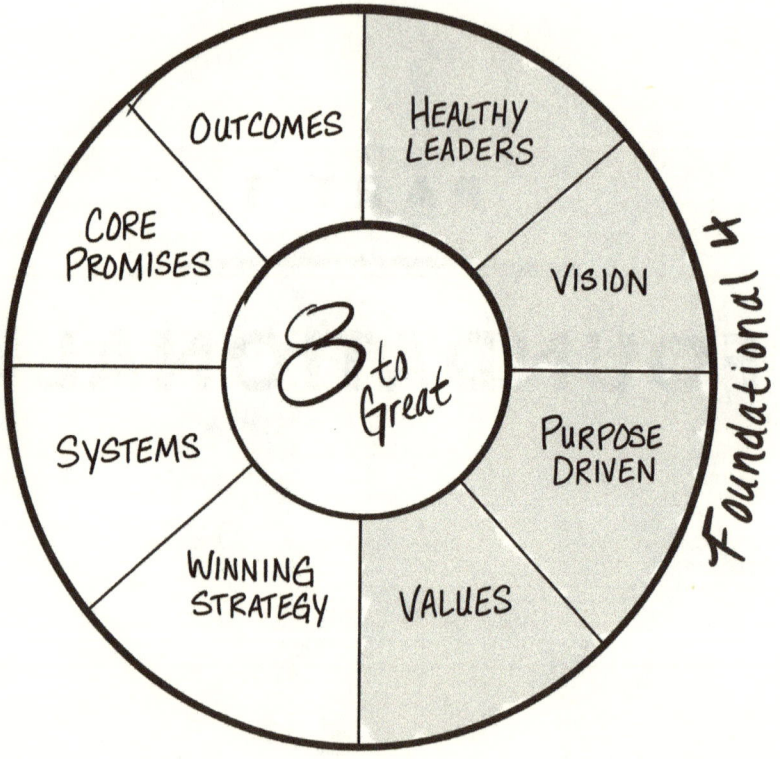

The foundation of any thriving business. If companies are not built on these 4 main components, they will inevitably starve the best version of themselves. Many businesses have made millions without these 4 components alive and integrated, but ultimately, they were what they forged—a cog in the machine. Nothing special, a mere wrinkle in a period of time. You deserve better; you owe it to yourself.

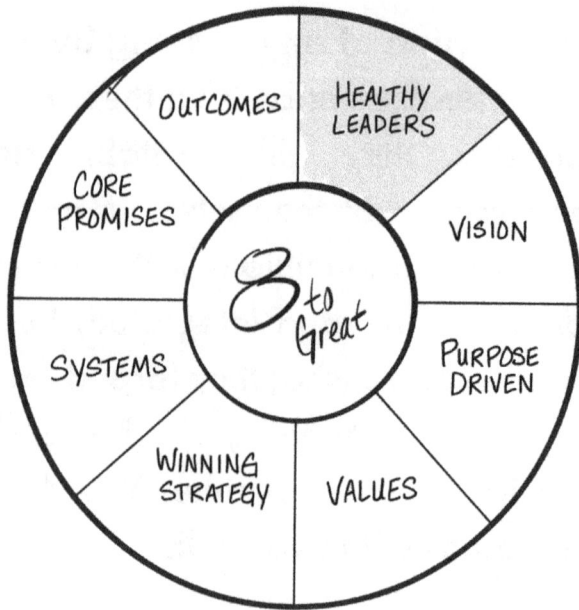

OUTCOMES

HEALTHY LEADERS

CORE PROMISES

VISION

SYSTEMS

8 to Great

PURPOSE DRIVEN

WINNING STRATEGY

VALUES

ONE

WHAT HEALTHY LEADERSHIP LOOKS LIKE

Focus on What Matters Most

"Really great people make you feel
that you, too, can become great."

—MARK TWAIN

"H E'S THE KIND OF MANAGER that every business dreams of."

Have you ever had that unstoppable high performer in your business? The one who seems to push through obstacles, and deliver results? I've seen many over the years, but one in particular I remember—I'll call him Mike. He was a senior-level employee with 15 years under his belt. Mike had a lot of knowledge, and the president loved him. He was relentless, the kind of guy who thrived on pressure and never backed down from a challenge.

First in, last out. He played a key role in launching new initiatives that brought in big revenue. If something needed fixed, Mike was on it. If a project was failing, he'd turn it around. To those watching from the outside, he looked like the perfect leader: an unstoppable, results-driven force to be reckoned with.

Beneath the surface, there was a different story. His team admired his work ethic but felt invisible in his shadow. They didn't feel heard or valued. Mike rarely checked in unless it was about a deadline or deliverable. Meetings were one way, where Mike talked, and everyone else listened. When his team spoke up, their ideas rarely gained traction. His peers barely noticed the problem because, on paper, Mike was a superstar. Even the leadership team, whether knowingly or not, seemed to ignore the cracks forming in his team.

BREAK THE CYCLE

The strangest part? This isn't an isolated story. Over lunch one day, a friend from another company told me about a similar experience. I've heard many more stories just like it from leaders over the years. This isn't simply a story about a high performer who doesn't know how to lead. It's a lesson about extremes. On one side, it's the bulldozer. On another, the data-obsessive, or even the people-using politician. Leading is more than doing or making progress, but often we get distracted by the big *shiny* numbers and think we're succeeding.

There's something more to leadership than that.

Leadership isn't *just* about profits, making decisions, driving results, or keeping the business afloat. Too many leaders are stuck in survival mode, reacting to daily chaos rather than shaping the future. They put out fires, manage crises, and push through each day with grit.

But real leadership isn't about managing the urgent; it's about building something that lasts.

This chapter is about breaking the cycle of managing everything and focusing on what delivers true results. It will give you the foundational clarity you need. You'll learn how to step out of the whirlwind and into leadership that creates lasting impact. True leadership is about cultivating a culture where people grow, excel, and push the business forward.

By the end of this chapter, you'll have a clear road map for stepping into Healthy Leadership. You'll understand how to shift from reactive to intentional, how to create clarity for your people, and how to develop habits that bring long-term stability. You might even have these principles already integrated, so I will give you new ways to digest and apply them. You'll walk away with key insights and ways to grow, no matter where your leadership is today.

THE LEADERSHIP GUT CHECK

We can define leadership in many ways, like the people overseeing teams, departments, and large projects in your company. It can be those who make big decisions, have influence, and are the last line of defense for your business. The people who are leading others are a direct reflection of your company, because they represent how you think, act, and respond. Building on this, is the concept of Healthy Leadership—the foundation of the 8 to Great framework, which is best defined with a question: Are you the ceiling or the door? The obstacle or the opportunity?

Most of us probably don't think of ourselves as being the obstacle that people might be facing. We tend to think more about the external obstacles we all face like *other* people: time, money, and all the restraints that flow between those. In reality, we are often one of the obstacles that people or our business faces, because we all have different personalities and perspectives. We are all *trying* to navigate human relationships. That is where the question comes in. In our relationships, are we creating barriers or obstacles as the ceiling, or opening a path to growth as the door?

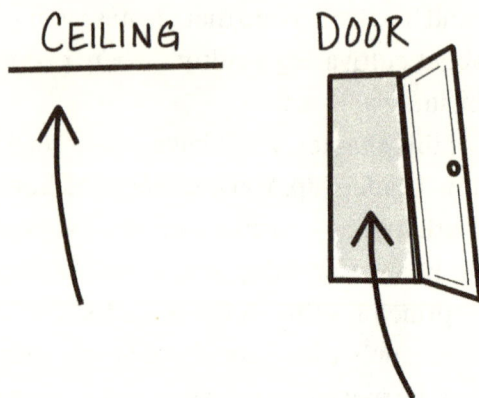

CEILING   DOOR

We've all heard it before: "That's their ceiling." A trusty metaphor for describing someone else's capacity. But it's not just about *their* potential. Sometimes, that ceiling is *your* doing. As a leader, you might be the one deciding just how high your team can go. Often, you're doing it without even realizing it. You're thinking, *Oh, they need a few more years before they're ready for that role.* Do they? Or is it possible you're projecting your own climb onto their journey? Maybe *you* needed a few years back in the day, so it just feels natural to assume they'll need the same.

But here's the twist: they *shouldn't* need as much time. Why? Because you (trailblazer that you are) cleared the path for them. Your hard work laid the foundation, so they can sprint where you had to crawl. That's the whole point of leadership, isn't it?

Still, let's be real for a second. There's a teeny, tiny part of us as leaders that clings to our role as *the seasoned pro.* Deep down, we might think, *Surely, this employee with less experience, fewer credentials, or not-as-many coffee-fueled all-nighters couldn't possibly be ready to do what I do. I've been at this for years.* But what if they *are* ready? Here's the uncomfortable truth: sometimes, we're not just the ceiling—we're the *padlock* on the door to greater opportunities. It's not about malice or jealousy; it's human nature.

Every leader should be the door. Maybe you haven't heard this one as a metaphor before, but we know exactly what a door does when it's opened. It allows us access to the other side. Often, it is the very thing that guides us to the unknown, a place with new opportunity. Opportunity to create, innovate, try something different, develop, and so much more. Every time a leader opens a door for someone else (gives opportunity), they also open the door for themselves to learn in a whole new way. Maybe they learn how to let go or possibly observe a new way to achieve something.

But what if you're *not* the ceiling? What if it's them?

KNOW WHO'S READY—AND WHO'S NOT

I'm not oblivious to the fact that some within your company simply can't walk through the door, even if you open it for them. In fact, you've probably tried with many people over the years, with no such luck. If you follow a typical performance distribution plot, you might relate to these standard numbers:

- 2% aren't hitting the mark; they just can't make it according to your standards and expectations.
- 14% are below average.
- 68% keep the lights on. These are the people who show up and mostly, do their job.
- 14% are above average.
- 2% are high performers helping build company success.

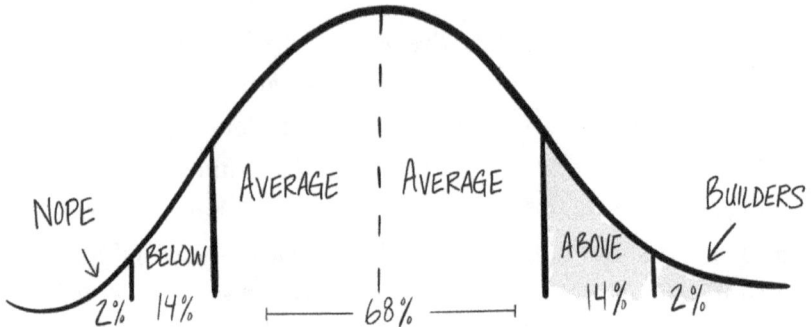

The truth is, being the ceiling or the door is about you, as much it is about them. There are always 2 sides to the coin. Understanding this, helps build a company where Healthy Leaders are held accountable for their part, just as much as employees are held accountable for theirs. We should concentrate on building the *above average* as Healthy Leaders. This will enable your business to begin growing, investing, and guiding the 68%.

WHEN THE PROBLEM ISN'T THE TEAM; IT'S THE LEADER

We were working with a business that had one particular manager, we'll call him Ted, with a team that kept performing terribly. Months would go by with multiple mistakes, some costing the company thousands of dollars. The president would ask, "What the heck is going on with your team?"

The president was confused because Ted was a great performer. He had led the company in sales, but his team wasn't clicking. Perplexed, the president reluctantly granted Ted the ability to hire another employee in hopes they just needed a higher performer. Ted found his gold mine of a person, with many years in the same industry, and hired her. Six months later, that high performer struggled. She got acclimated quickly and started off great, but then, fell on her face.

What happened?

I always go straight to the top with problems. They might appear somewhere down the line in the company, but the root of any consistent issue should be dealt with at the leadership level.

The problem was Ted. He was slow to hold people accountable. He gave greenlights to people without asking the right questions and rarely checked their work. When I met with his *high-performing* new employee, she revealed that she needed someone who kept her on track and gave guidance. And that wasn't Ted.

Was it her fault? No, she needed to be managed like 68% of most employees.

Ted was a high performer, but he wasn't a Healthy Leader. He was promoted on *what* he did, but not for *who* he was as a leader. Ted was focused on doing *his* daily work. He rarely held his team accountable, had zero processes in place for training, and didn't spend time helping them solve issues. Ted was stuck on the wrong side of the leadership dichotomy.

THE HEALTHY LEADERSHIP DICHOTOMY

Leaders will have a pull between 2 extremes that will never be in perfect balance. It is a constant battle for your yes in either direction. The first direction is the negative (–), which is what we are fighting against. This happens when we get caught in the Dismal Daily and become Me Focused.

Dismal Daily (–)

The Dismal Daily is the constant grind, the whirlwind that sweeps you away from what is important and keeps you from getting back. It's the tide that sucks you down, the fires that need to be put out too often. Though a lot of tasks and responsibilities are necessary for success, they can overshadow other areas of leadership. It's far too easy to get stuck in the Dismal Daily for a variety of reasons. Maybe you like to be busy, appreciate feeling needed, or haven't figured out how to empower your team well. Or possibly, you're in a season of peak workload. I'm not saying that it can't happen. I'm saying you can't stay there. When leaders say they don't have enough time to focus on things like long-term goals or they only have time to do the urgent work to keep the company afloat, they haven't grasped Parkinson's Law. It states, your responsibilities and tasks will expand to fill the time you give to complete them. It's about what you're *picking* to put on your list, not that you don't have enough time.

Here's an example to help prove the relevance. One of our clients was overseeing many functions of his business like sales, finance, and even doing some of the physical work. At this point in our time together, he had built a $4 million business with long-lasting customers. When I asked him why he had not empowered someone else to take over these functions of the business, he simply said, "I don't have time to train someone." You get where this is going.

Within 2 months, we had audited where his time was going and how much of it was in each function of the business. First, we tracked it by hours, then by minutes. Each week, I asked if he could do those tasks in half the time. He would laugh and say, "Maybe." He was competitive, so I would triple dog dare him to give it a shot. Of course, that worked. What we found was astonishing. Well, not really...Each week within that 2-month span, he would actually do the tasks in half the time. After those 2 months, he started to train someone on finance and sales.

The point is, we often will expand our time to the tasks or responsibilities we think we should be doing. If you give yourself 2 hours to do something, guess how long it will take? You guessed it, 2 hours.

This isn't just a story about him though—it's a story about all of us. We often get stuck in the Dismal Daily (–), but as this story shows us, there is a way out.

Each of us should review and plan our time to stay out of the constant whirlwind as leaders. Ask these questions to assess your Dismal Daily. Use them and your average workweek as a guide to plan:

1. What percentage of my time should I dedicate each week to *doing the work*?
2. What percentage of my time should I dedicate each week to helping my team?
3. What percentage should I dedicate each week to have blocked-off time for getting caught up?

Me Focused (–)

The second pull to the negative (–), Me Focused, is exactly what it sounds like. Not every leader will know they are too focused on themselves. We all need reflection and feedback to know where we stand. Still, we know it's *not* hard to get stuck on our own issues. Me Focused is the second negative pulling us in the wrong direction. It's a trap that leads to a long road of self-centered, unsatisfied, and ungrateful attitudes.

Ask these questions to assess your Me Focus:

1. Am I prioritizing my team's development and success over my personal recognition?
2. Do I listen more than I speak during conversations with my team?
3. Am I more concerned about being right or achieving the best outcome?

Don't assess this on your own. It's best to have vulnerable, 1-on-1 discussions with your team. Even if they don't tell you the hard truth the first time, every time you ask, you will be building trust with them. Over time, if you are intentionally and humbly asking, you will get true feedback.

Together, the Dismal Daily and being Me Focused make up an everyday fight that we encounter as leaders.

The other extreme, the path in the opposite direction, is the one we should all strive to be on.

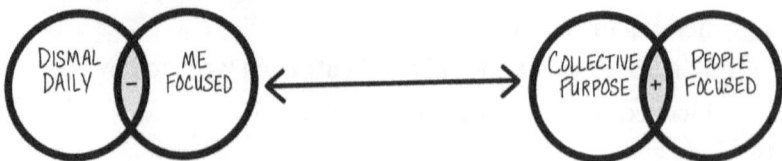

Collective Purpose (+)

The journey toward the positive (+) direction is rooted in 2 key principles: Collective Purpose and being People Focused.

At its core, Collective Purpose means clarifying the *why* at every level—individual, team, and business. It's about rallying around a shared vision and moving in a direction that only a united group can achieve. Every project, task, and responsibility contributes to fulfilling a larger goal. However, achieving Collective Purpose isn't automatic. It requires intentionality, a deep sense of meaning, and relentless dedication to the greater good. To be clear, we're not saying ignore yourself, but most of us already default to focusing inward. Left unchecked, this self-concern can quickly become unhealthy. People Focused pairs with Collective Purpose and is about concentrating on your people, wanting to see them win more than anything.

People Focused (+)

By intentionally practicing the discipline of focusing on others, leaders build stronger teams and develop themselves more rapidly in the process. This is counterintuitive. It's a paradoxical idea rooted in pure observation. It's like teaching someone a craft. Even though you know it really well, when you teach someone else, you iron out your own skills even more. You learn to share something in the moment, and in return, you're more equipped than before.

This balance, turning outward while resisting self-centered leadership, is the essential first step in a much larger journey. But even as leaders begin focusing on people and development, one major ingredient is often missing: alignment. Without alignment, even the most well-intentioned leaders fall flat.

GET EVERYONE ON THE SAME PAGE...FINALLY

One of the most common challenges I see, regardless of whether a business is just getting started or has been around for decades, is a lack of shared understanding among leaders about what the business actually does, who it serves, and how it delivers value.

Healthy Leadership requires alignment. Truly effective leaders have an unwavering understanding of who the business serves and how it delivers value to them. When leaders know their target customers and their needs, it shapes decision-making, drives focus, and ensures that every team member understands the bigger picture. This alignment transforms your business from a collection of disconnected tasks into a cohesive force working toward shared goals.

Knowing who your business helps requires more than identifying a target market. It's about deeply understanding your customers' needs, pain points, and aspirations.

- **Who are they?** Describe your ideal customer beyond demographics—what's their role, mindset, and industry?
- **What do they value most?** This digs deeper into their priorities: speed, quality, trust, innovation, etc.
- **What problems are they actively trying to solve?** Focus on pain points that are urgent or costly enough to take action on.
- **What's getting in their way?** Identify the internal or external barriers keeping them from solving their problem.
- **How does your business uniquely help them?** Clarify how your offering fits into their goals or makes their life easier. What's the real impact?

Leaders should prioritize finding answers to these questions and embedding that knowledge into the company's culture. A leadership team aligned on this creates a ripple effect. When everyone knows your what, who, and how, it fosters intentionality in every interaction, from sales to customer service to execution.

Ambiguity in this area breeds inefficiency and confusion. Alignment must start with your leaders and permeate throughout the front line. It must be part of onboarding, training, and performance development. Every position, from marketing to operations, should be able to articulate who the business serves and how it helps them. When this alignment is achieved, it creates a shared sense of purpose, stronger collaboration, and a company culture rooted in serving customers effectively.

When Growth Gets Fuzzy

A friend of mine, John, founded his architecture firm many years ago. His vision was simple: to design beautiful, functional spaces that enhanced communities. But as the firm gained traction, John found himself saying yes to every opportunity. Soon, his team was juggling residential projects, commercial builds, interior design, and even landscaping. They expanded into new markets without a clear strategy, from luxury homes to retail spaces and corporate offices.

The excitement of growth turned into frustration. Employees were constantly learning new design software, adapting to different project scopes, and struggling to meet the expectations of wildly diverse clients. His business lacked clarity of its ideal customer, taking on any project that came through the door. The breaking point came when a commercial project had some missed deadlines and quality issues, which led to a major loss in revenue that year.

When we stripped back the layers of their overcomplicated business, through whiteboard sessions and deep discussions, we discovered their unique strength: designing community-centric spaces with an emphasis on small businesses. It was the following question that helped the most: How does your business solve your customers' problems in ways others cannot?

They discovered that the biggest *hole* in the market was something they could do very well. Everyone was chasing the huge projects, but the small businesses were underserved. They had many clients give them feedback that they were turned away from other firms because of their workload. This gave the team clarity. Employees were more focused and were able to do a few things really well. This was a valuable lesson—ultimately proving that narrowing their focus was the foundation for true growth.

John's story is a powerful reminder of how easy it is to drift away from clarity in the pursuit of growth. But gaining clarity isn't *just* about refining target customers; it's also about investing in people. As mentioned earlier, the positive (+) focus is Collective Purpose and People Focused. This is where the Healthy Leader's GIG (Grow, Invest, Guide) framework comes in. It ensures leaders are actively cultivating growth. This next part dives deeper into what it means to be People Focused.

THE HEALTHY LEADER'S GIG

The growth of a company will only be as fruitful as the knowledge and desired behaviors that are passed on. Every leader should be willing to truly develop the people that they have been given the opportunity to lead. Harvey Firestone, founder of Firestone Tire and Rubber Company, said, "It's only when we develop others that we permanently succeed." The culture of developing others shouldn't be a choice. Simply put, all leaders in your company should be accountable for the GIG. This is the heart of Healthy Leadership. When people feel valued and equipped, they take ownership, solve problems more effectively, and drive innovation. This creates scalability—allowing your business to grow beyond you. Instead of being the bottleneck, you become the catalyst for sustainable success.

When was the last time you met someone who went out of their way and gave up their time freely? They truly focused on others. How many people came to mind? Probably not a lot—most of us are busy moving and shaking, probably even doing too much. Your employees will follow those who invest in them. In return, this builds a business that people want to be a part of, not just work for.

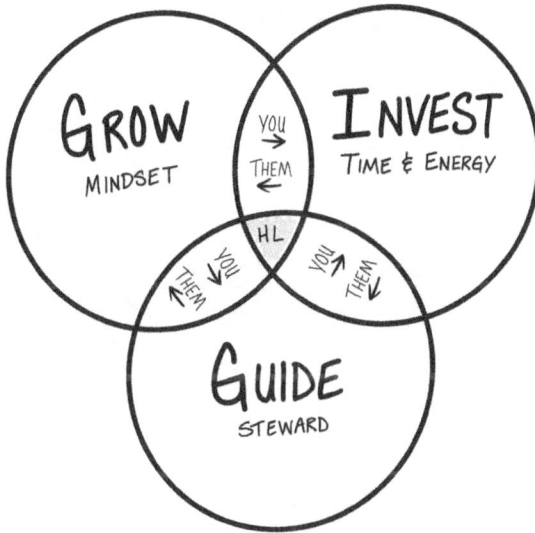

The 3 parts of GIG—Grow, Invest, Guide—are reliant on each other. They can't be separated, left on their own, or chosen individually based on what fits you best. GIG is also twofold. Each part is not only development for the people around you, but also development for you. You must practice what you preach when it comes to developing others. Consider a physical trainer. You wouldn't want to take advice from a trainer who was in the same shape or worse than you. You want someone who has a proven success record, and it shows. Likewise, if you aren't developing yourself and show-ing the outputs, then you will have less influence with the people around you.

First, Grow

Grow is about your mindset. A growing mindset is the belief that talents, skills, and intelligence can be developed with effort, learn-ing, and persistence. It is not just about talent; it's about how you approach challenges and opportunities for growth. At its core, a growing mindset is built on 3 essential components: **Ability**, **Awareness**, and **Improvement**. These elements work together to shape an individual's capacity to learn, adapt, and excel in any area of life.

1. Ability: Recognizing Your Strengths

Ability is the foundation of a growing mindset. It represents the natural talents, skills, and knowledge you already possess. Everyone has unique abilities, but the key is to recognize and embrace them. While ability provides the starting point, a growing mindset means understanding that talent alone isn't enough—what you do with your abilities deter-mines success. Helping your people recognize their ability is dif-ferent, though. Have you ever had someone tell you that you were great at something? I remember when my good friend Nick told me that my drawings were powerful. I drew things all the time for cli-ents, but I never thought of it as a strength. But when Nick told me that they were powerful and it would be irresponsible not to draw more of them for people, I was blown away. He had recognized an ability that I knew I had, but it didn't come to life until he shared

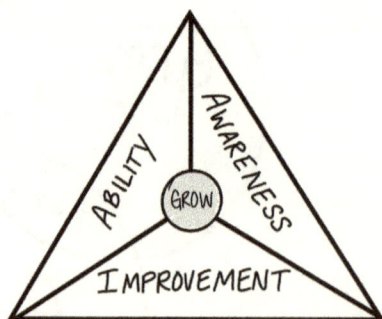

how I could use it. A growing mindset isn't just about knowing your strengths; it's also about speaking life into others and sharing what you believe their strengths are. It's irresponsible not to do this for your team. Thank you to the Nicks of the world.

2. Awareness: Understanding Your Potential and Gaps

Awareness is the bridge between ability and improvement. It involves self-reflection, recognizing where you excel, and identifying areas that need to be developed. Without awareness, even the most talented individuals can become stagnant. Cultivating awareness means seeking feedback, being open to constructive criticism, and understanding that learning is a continuous process. It allows individuals to pinpoint weaknesses without fear and see them as opportunities rather than limitations. Have you experienced someone who got defensive when another person gave them feedback? What happens next? That person vows to never give them feedback again, or worse, they only give them good feedback from that time forward. Awareness is about creating a culture where barriers are broken down and people truly want feedback. They want to know where they can improve. Helping others to gain awareness can be as simple as the leader going first and sharing where they think they have room for improvement. This breeds a culture where others want to gain more self-awareness, so they can improve.

3. Improvement: Taking Action

Improvement is the driving force that transforms awareness into real progress. It's the active pursuit of learning, practice, and refinement. Those with a growing mindset embrace challenges, put in the effort to develop new skills, and persist despite obstacles. Improvement requires discipline, adaptability, and resilience, continuously pushing beyond comfort zones to achieve new levels of success. Helping others improve means that what gets discussed gets put down on paper. Without a plan being communicated and shared, improvement will just be a distant thought. Taking action means there is intentionality with a written plan for you and them. Sharing your own plan will accelerate how well you can help others with theirs.

These 3 elements—Ability, Awareness, and Improvement—are interconnected to form the first *G*, Grow. Ability provides the foundation, Awareness guides direction, and Improvement ensures ongoing growth. Together, they form what's needed to unlock potential, embrace challenges, and achieve long-term success.

Grow: You Still Matter More Than You Think

Years ago, I worked with a well-known leader in our community, the president of a high-quality manufacturing company who had built his business from scratch. By the time we partnered with his company, they had tripled in both revenue and workforce. But beneath all the success, the president had started to believe a subtle yet dangerous lie, "I don't have anything valuable to offer anymore." He'd convinced himself that his team, armed with their new computer skills and cutting-edge methods, had far surpassed anything he could contribute. This mindset began to creep into his leadership, undermining his confidence.

Over the course of a year, we worked with him to rewrite these unhelpful *soundbites* playing on repeat. This wasn't about reinventing the wheel. It was about reminding him that the grit, perseverance, and faith that built the business were not just quaint relics of the past—they were timeless principles that still held immense value. Sure, the methods of work had evolved, but the core ingredients for success—talent, grit, and a willingness to adapt—never go out of style. We encouraged him to share his history, lessons learned, and guiding principles with his team. These conversations became cherished by his employees, not only for the team but also for the president himself. Growth isn't about knowing all the answers. It's about embracing the right mindset and leveraging your unique story.

Second, Invest

The *I*, in the GIG, stands for Invest. As with all sections of the GIG, it is equally important to invest in yourself *and* the team. Invest is defined by the giving of your time and your energy. Imagine you have endless time to sit down with your team and really invest in their future. You spend countless hours each day just being next to them. Sound crazy? That's because it is. I have not run across one leader, to date, that has time on their side. Sure, we hear about those people working on the beach somewhere. However, back here, on planet Earth, that's not reality for 99%. We are striving to find another minute and trying to keep up with the fires of yesterday, maybe even from a year ago. I get it. I understand the tension, but investing your time is like exercising. You can find 1,000 excuses for why you can't do it. And, even when you dig deep and do it, you won't see immediate results. This is the reality of investing your time.

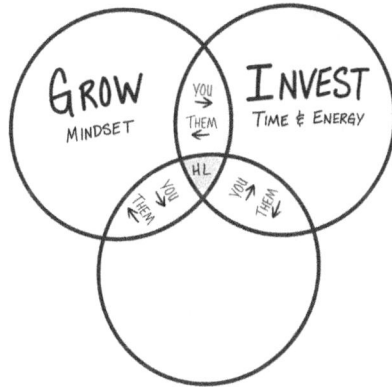

Don't forget it's time *and* energy. I once worked with a guy, let's call him Brad. Brad was a mover and shaker. He had all the energy in the world. Brad would zip by offices, shout out a few things and give a few words of wisdom, but never slowed down to genuinely invest in the people around him. Eventually, his team members began to notice his pattern and lack of time to help them. This pattern reared its head in my direction as well. One day, I had an important question for him. He came zipping by. I caught him and asked if he would mind giving me a few minutes to discuss a project with him. "Sure thing!" he said, which was immediately followed by, "But I'm leaving right now. How about a call as soon as I hop in the truck?" I agreed, and after waiting about 5 minutes, I called him. I was met with the annoying sound of him on the other line. And that was that. I never even discussed the project with him—no time!

Energy must be paired with time. On the flip side, you've probably also experienced someone who has all the time in the world but no energy. Not good...nap time! Investing takes both. But don't forget, investing in yourself is just as important as it is for other people. You must learn to give time and energy for your own development. If you don't, neither will your team. They will mimic what you do.

I remember when I first started working for a small business after college, the office manager would take a 15-minute lunch break. As I began to notice, so did everyone else in the office, and it wasn't too long before I fell in line and did the same, scarfing down my food every day. If you don't give yourself time and energy to invest in you, neither will your team. They will follow your behavior and actions. Invest in both you and your people.

Third, Guide

Let's start with a clarification—guiding is different from telling or directing. Developing people requires us to give our perspective without telling them exactly how to do something or take control. Guide, the ending *G* in the GIG, is a 2-way street just like the other 2 components. While there is development happening for your people, there is also development happening for you. It's a *stretching* process for both sides that requires restraint. You can probably relate to the expression "I can just do it myself faster (or insert better... or both, ha!)."

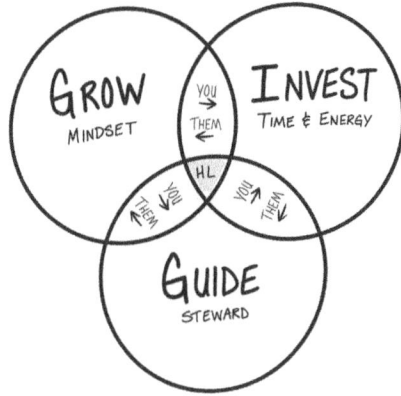

Of course you can, but that isn't how the GIG works. You can't just do the tasks and solve all the problems. That only helps in the short-term, and even then, your team will feel held back. They will become your shadow. Obviously, this doesn't mean you shouldn't give good direction or in some cases, complete the task to mitigate risk, but when you are intentionally guiding, you help problem solve while allowing for learning through some potential mistakes. Stewarding, through guidance, requires the leader to put *safety nets* in place, mitigating the chance for failing miserably, but allowing for learning.

Far too often we believe we need to be right on the heels of our team, masking this behavior with the word *accountability*. Yes, delegation should work hand in hand with accountability. The problem is, leaders often have a tendency to hide behind accountability, when in reality, it's our control that we can't relinquish. On the other hand, avoidance isn't accountability either. I'll spare you the many examples we have. I'm sure you could insert one of your own, but the bottom line is, we can't *empower* someone and then avoid them, pretending or assuming they don't need our guidance.

Contrastingly, guiding requires that we take risks by providing the right opportunities, and check-in along the way to steward the relationship. It's not just giving them the things we don't want to do but rather allowing them to take on new responsibilities. These might be hard words to hear, but it's not uncommon to see both sides of control and avoidance being a mask for empowerment and accountability.

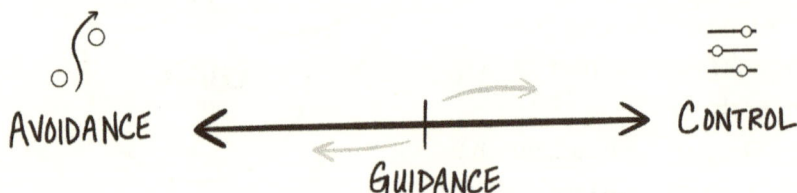

AVOIDANCE ⟵————————⟶ CONTROL

GUIDANCE

Somewhere in the middle, between avoidance and control, is guidance. In order to empower well, leaders need to learn the delicate balance of letting go and guiding. Guidance is the ability to delegate responsibilities and tasks paired with the right amount of stewarding and accountability.

Guide: If You Grip Too Tight, They'll Let Go

One manager stands out for teaching a lesson in the importance of guiding. The shocking part, given the great company he was in, is that this was a lesson in what *not* to do. This manager was a 20-year vet for the company and had a seat next to the CEO nearly his entire career. He was particular. Well, that's what he called it. There were a lot of variables here, but the reality was that his micromanagement was overwhelming. Regardless, he grew his team and had a standout employee. Every time I talked to this employee, he would mention the control of his manager, saying, "I love this place, but man, that guy just likes to breathe down my neck!" What kept him there? Well, I think it was the company's overall culture, until it wasn't enough.

When he received an offer with a 10% salary increase, he jumped at it without much hesitation, even though he was slated to take his manager's position within a few years, which at this company, could have been a 30% increase in pay at minimum. It wasn't that he didn't have the foresight to see his success and opportunity—he was just done. The manager's controlling behavior was so daunting that he wasn't willing to stick around a few years under the same conditions. Guiding is allowing your team to explore new skills, learn with some accountability, and ultimately become the best problem solvers. Guiding is not controlling, nor is it avoiding.

THE GIG MOMENTUM

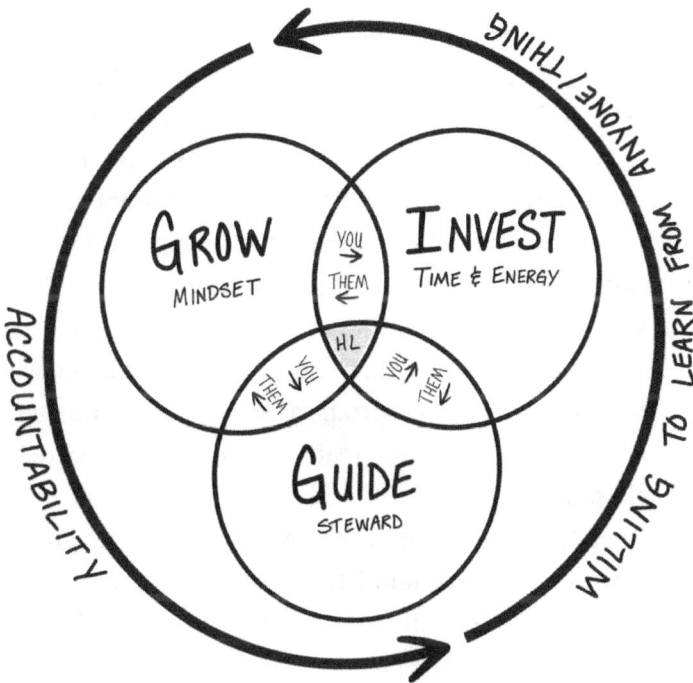

As we've explored, the GIG is about building up people that help grow your business, beyond one or a few. The GIG is how I've helped many businesses and seen them scale effectively, but to truly propel your business forward, you need momentum. You can only get true traction on the GIG if you incorporate these 2 core principles:

1. Be willing to learn from anyone and anything
2. Accountability

These 2 essentials create the necessary momentum to break free from the gravitational pull of being Me Focused (–).

And let's be honest—pulling away from that selfish orbit isn't easy. Notice how the arrows in the GIG visual spin *counter*-clockwise. That's no accident. Learning and accountability run counter to what comes naturally for most of us. It's far more comfortable to stick to what we know and remain in our own echo chamber.

Let's dive into the first principle: *being willing to learn from anyone and anything*. This requires an openness that keeps us in a perpetual posture of giving while remaining humble enough to receive. It's easy to say, "I'll never stop learning," but how often do we really act on that sentiment? How often do we look for lessons in people we don't agree with, in uncomfortable situations, or even in failure? That's the kicker—learning doesn't come with an off switch. True growth comes from the messy, awkward, and even frustrating moments where you learn something unexpected from an unlikely source.

Then there's *accountability*, the less glamorous yet absolutely essential side of the equation. Let's be clear: real accountability is not a casual *check-in* with a friend who will nod and agree. No, true accountability requires vulnerability, honesty, and consistency. It means surrounding yourself with people who will tell you the truth, even when it stings. But it's not just about having someone to hold *you* accountable. It's also about you being willing to do the same for others. Accountability is a 2-way street, built on mutual trust and shared commitment. Think of accountability as the guardrails that keep you from veering off course. Without it, we naturally drift toward what's easy or comfortable, often at the expense of what's needed. These 2 principles are non-negotiables. They're the engine of the GIG and the tools that keep us moving in the right direction.

UNHEALTHY LEADERSHIP

Unhealthy leadership often stems from a Me Focused mindset, where leaders get so tangled in their own to-do lists, emails, and never-ending Zoom meetings that they forget there's a team out there counting on them. This self-centered approach isn't necessarily because leaders lack charisma or are scheming in some way. It's often just the by-product of being stuck in the Dismal Daily (−). Leaders trapped in this hamster wheel can get overwhelmed by putting out fires, chasing details, and clinging to their own corner of chaos. They inadvertently create a vacuum where the focus shifts inward—on their own survival, ambition, or ego—while their team is left feeling unseen, unsupported, and unappreciated. This is not always on purpose. We all gravitate toward something within our personalities. That's why it's so important to embrace the GIG.

The reality is unhealthy leadership isn't about lacking a sparkling personality. It's about failing to focus on others, while balancing the development of yourself. This inward focus can lead to decisions based on self-preservation rather than shared progress, the Collective Purpose (+).

Hitting the Gig Mark?

Reading the last 2 paragraphs, you might have thought, *That's not me!* You're not some unhealthy leader completely focused on yourself. Often, it's not the people who blatantly disregard others that I see as the biggest threat to Healthy Leadership—it's the ones who give *just* enough. The ones who often fly under the radar. Their teams will know you're leaving something on the table. Their employees will know but often won't say anything. They'll just leave when they have the first opportunity. If you're not fully immersed into Healthy Leadership, they will know and feel it.

Flying under the radar is kind of like physical health—you exercise (sometimes) and eat *right*, but for some reason, you aren't in the shape you want to be. For most of us in this boat, we might not be fully committed. Maybe we have too many cheat meals or sleep-in one too many times. There's something missing. Maybe this correlates with your leadership or others leading in your company. These are the leaders we want to find and help the most. Identifying them is challenging but is worth the effort.

I'll pause here for a second and say, these *fly-under-the-radar* leaders might not know they aren't quite hitting the mark with the GIG. Here are some questions to help you identify and assist them:

THE GIG MARK QUESTIONNAIRE

Use this rating scale. At the end, find which side they land on the most, (–) or the (+):

1. Never (–)
2. Sometimes (–)
3. Mostly (+)
4. Yes (+)

Grow: Mindset

1. Do they actively seek opportunities for personal and professional growth?
2. Are they self-aware, openly acknowledging their strengths and development opportunities?

---

3. Do they coach and develop their team members to improve their skills?

4. Can they adapt and pivot based on feedback and new challenges?

5. Do they hold themselves accountable for continuous learning and progress?

Invest: Time and Energy

1. Do they dedicate focused time to developing their team members, beyond just quick check-ins?

2. Do they bring energy and engagement when investing in their team, rather than just going through the motions?

3. Are they intentional about their own personal and professional growth, setting an example for their team?

4. Do they balance urgency and availability, ensuring they don't rush interactions or neglect important conversations?

5. Do their team members feel supported, valued, and confident in their leader's commitment to their success?

Guide: Steward

1. Do they empower employees to make decisions and take ownership of their work rather than micromanaging?

2. Do they provide clear expectations and accountability without creating a culture of fear or excessive control?

3. Do they support employee growth by allowing team members to take on challenges and learn from mistakes?

4. Do they balance oversight with trust, ensuring employees feel guided rather than controlled or avoided?

5. Would their team members say they feel valued, trusted, and encouraged?

People Build the Business;
Leaders Build the People

As your business scales, the need for strong, people-focused leadership becomes paramount. Growth inevitably brings increased complexity, higher stakes, and a larger team to manage. Without a solid foundation of Healthy Leadership, cracks will start to show in employee engagement, customer satisfaction, and ultimately, your bottom line. You may not see it right away—but it will affect your bottom line.

The principles we've explored in this chapter—developing a growing mindset, investing time and energy into your people, and providing empowering guidance—are not just *nice-to-haves* for aspiring leaders. They are the essential components for building a self-sustaining business.

Conversely, leaders who neglect the human side of the equation in pursuit of pure results will find their growth stalling or even reversing. No matter how impressive your products or services may be, they will always be limited by the people powering them.

WIN THEIR HEARTS,
THEN SHOW THEM THE WAY

From an unknown wisdom source, "People won't remember what you said, but they will remember how you made them feel." We all know when someone truly is balancing the GIG or not. It's our sixth sense. If you want others to follow where you're taking them, they must first trust and follow you and the leaders you put in place. Only then will they follow your vision.

Vision isn't just about the near future; it's also about the long term, the journey a decade ahead. If you want people to stay with your company for the long game, then have a compelling vision that is built on Healthy Leaders. In the next chapter, we will discuss the key elements of Vision and how many have missed 1 of the greatest opportunities within their business and future.

TAKE-IT-WITH-YOU NOTE

The growth of a company will only be as fruitful as the knowledge and desired behaviors that are passed on. Every leader should be willing to truly develop the people that they have been given the opportunity to lead and embrace the Healthy Leadership GIG.

BONUS: CHICAGO BULLS, ALL HEART

On March 28, 1990, Michael Jordan delivered one of the greatest performances in NBA history, scoring an incredible **69 points** in the Bulls' 117-113 overtime win against the Cavaliers. Rookie Stacey King, the Bulls' sixth overall pick from the 1989 draft, contributed just **1 point** that night. After the game, when reporters asked King about Jordan's historic night, he quipped, "I'll always remember this as the night that Michael and I combined for 70 points." It was a hilarious and humble comment that has since become a legendary piece of Bulls history.

King's funny moment reflects a powerful truth about leadership. Just like Jordan put in the work to make history, great leaders lay the foundation for success and create space for others to share in it. Healthy Leadership isn't about taking all the credit—it's about empowering those around you, giving them the confidence and opportunity to contribute, and recognizing the value of every role. True leadership is knowing that while you may carry the weight, the victory is shared.

WHY HEALTHY LEADERSHIP?

1. Healthy Leaders are the foundation of scaling and building a business that doesn't depend on you.
2. The GIG is broken down into 3 parts: Grow, Invest, Guide, each one reliant on the others. They can't be separated, left on their own, or chosen individually based on what fits you best.
3. Willing to learn from anyone/thing and accountability is what drives the GIG of Healthy Leaders.

CAUTION

1. One of the most common challenges is a lack of shared understanding among leaders about what the business actually does, who it serves, and how it delivers value.
2. Unhealthy leadership often stems from a Me Focused mindset, where leaders get so tangled in their own to-do lists, emails, and never-ending Zoom meetings that they forget there's a team out there counting on them.
3. Avoidance is not accountability, and neither is control. Guidance is the ability to delegate responsibilities and tasks paired with the right amount of oversight.

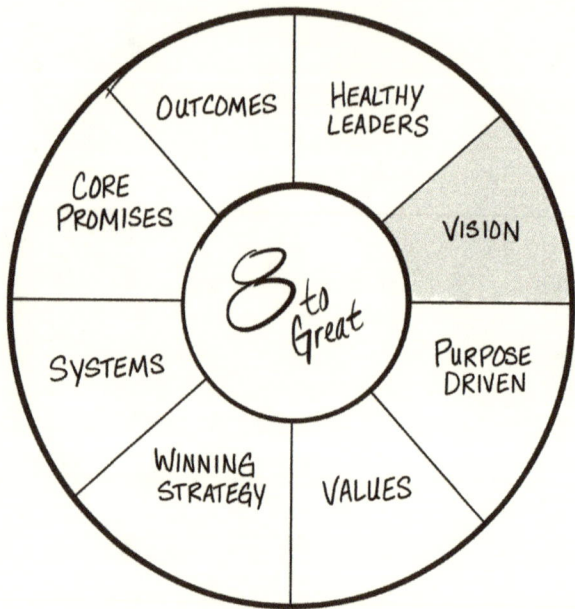

OUTCOMES

HEALTHY LEADERS

CORE PROMISES

VISION

SYSTEMS

8 to Great

PURPOSE DRIVEN

WINNING STRATEGY

VALUES

TWO

CRAFT A COMPELLING VISION

Create a Future Your People Want

"You can't depend on your eyes when
your imagination is out of focus."
—MARK TWAIN

WHAT IF YOU COULD shake up an entire industry with a single, simple vision? That's exactly what Warby Parker did in 2010 when they set out to disrupt the eyewear market. At the time, glasses were ridiculously overpriced, with a handful of companies controlling the market and leaving customers with limited options. Warby Parker's founders saw a gap—and an opportunity. Their vision was simple but revolutionary: design their own frames, sell directly to consumers online, and make stylish, high-quality glasses affordable.

The real game-changer? Their Home Try-On program, where customers could try 5 frames at home and only buy what they loved. It was a direct challenge to the eyewear giants, and it worked.

But they envisioned a future that wasn't just about business; it was also about impact. For every pair of glasses sold, they committed to donating a pair to someone in need through their Buy a Pair, Give a Pair program. Warby Parker's story is proof that a clear, bold vision isn't just about driving sales. It's about creating, competing, and doing what others won't.

What you foresee as your future doesn't have to be this grand of an idea—it's actually practical and for the simple, hardworking, been-doing-this-for-40-years kind of companies. As in the Warby Parker story, it can start small, but if it's compelling, it won't stay small.

What separates true visionaries from the rest? It's not their ability to create something new; it's their relentless commitment to a future that others can't yet see. This is not just for big corporations; it's for everyday businesses down the street and around the corner.

As a business leader, at one point you probably were presented with the question, "What's your vision for your company?" If you're like me, you probably got practical and said something about revenue. You might have had the forethought to throw in some other things like more people, better equipment, maybe another location, etc. The word vision is funny like that—a lot of us revert to more operational and tactical things. Maybe you could even relate that you don't like the topic because it feels like it's for those people that want to change the world. I don't disagree that it feels like that, but I know without a doubt there's something so much more that we're missing when it comes to this topic. This chapter is about building a clear and inspiring vision: one that not only motivates your team but also guides decision-making and daily actions.

VISION ISN'T JUST A DREAM—IT'S DIRECTION

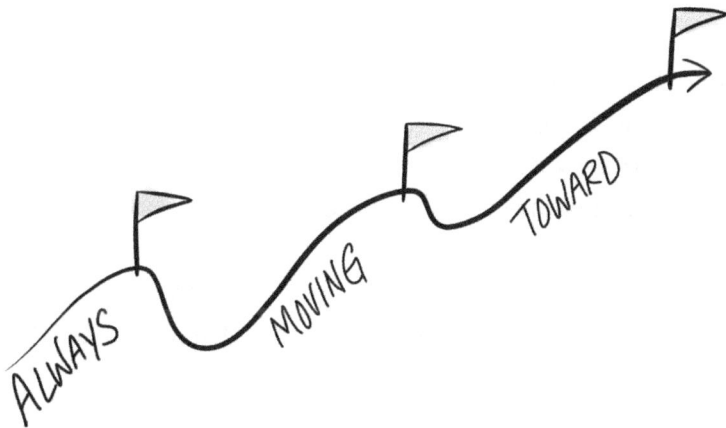

Simply stated, it's having a very clear, strong picture of what your business will look like in the future. This is the second component of 8 to Great, a vision that compels your leaders and teams toward something bigger than they can accomplish on their own.

It's not a fixed point on the map—it's a consistently evolving journey. The most influential leaders understand that vision is about continually moving forward.

In this chapter, you'll learn how to embrace that mindset, keeping your company focused on progress and inviting people on the journey. You'll discover practical steps to identify where you're headed, how to navigate the unknown, and what it takes to turn a distant dream into a tangible reality. More importantly, you'll learn how to align your team with it, ensuring that everyone is moving in the same direction with clarity. A vision that isn't shared isn't a vision at all; it's just an idea. By the end of this chapter, you'll have the tools to create one that's not only inspiring but also actionable, guiding your company forward with confidence and momentum.

ALWAYS AND HORIZON: THE 2 ANCHORS

There are 2 types that are a part of Vision. First, there is your Always Vision. This one's a bit counterintuitive, so I'll expand on this soon. Second, there is the Horizon Vision. This is just out of reach at the moment, but probably achievable within 3 to 5 years, both obtainable with strategy, dedication, and time. When thinking about the 2 parts of a compelling vision, remember to, *always* move toward the *horizon*. Your company cannot drive in the right direction without these 2 anchors. Later, we will discuss how both of these are the compass for your Winning Strategy as they define the direction of your company.

In my encounters with businesses of all different sizes, it's apparent that each of them has a belief attached to the word vision. Many use people like Elon Musk or Bill Gates to describe what it means. They start off by saying, "It's this radical state of the company's future. It's bold and daring." Taken back by the seeming intensity of their view of the word, they'd rather be a little bit more realistic, tangible, numerical, and practical. It can then become easy to skip over Vision and simply stick to yearly goals. Not every company is designed to be innovators, and to those that are not, it can be difficult to create and cascade your desired future. The issue is that most people in your business operate with an innate need to foresee what lies ahead. The good news is that there is a unique vision for every company, and every leader can develop their own. In fact, we are all more familiar with creating our future than we might realize.

You've Been *Envisioning* All Along

Picture this: you start your career as a twentysomething. You're ambitious. You have a lot of fight in you to do some good in this world and make some money along the way. As you're starting out,

someone asks, "What are your plans for your future?" You probably know the answer without putting too much thought into it.
You want to earn money, build a good future for your family, buy a
house, etc. Now, this might seem like a silly example, but as it illustrates, most of us are already working from a future vision we've
developed for ourselves. Typically, that future is not the same as it
is in the present. You aren't going to be living in an apartment with
your buddy Joe, eating pizza, and playing *Call of Duty* all your life.
You've given yourself some sort of future plans. Often, we don't call
this vision though—we call these goals. But Vision is a collection of
goals, characteristics, and desires, put together to create your outlook. Every company owes its employees the same thing, to give an
outlook of the company's future.

PART I: ALWAYS VISION

Driving towards your Always Vision doesn't come naturally for
most leaders. This requires that you articulate what your company will look like in 10+ years. This is not an arbitrary amount
of time. A decade is practical because it is a milestone for most
businesses. The best part about this type of vision is that it's
never-ending—it keeps adapting and being tweaked like a moving bullseye. Essentially, you continually run towards this, and
just when you think you've arrived, you realize you always have
more work to do, hints the *always* part. This vision is tied to big
milestones that almost seem impossible at the moment. For
many businesses, it means big revenue growth, team expansions,
acquisitions, and additional services or products. For others, it
might be about developing *deeper* as a company and improving their current operation. The Always Vision is not just about
these big goals, but also a desired future with some details for
further clarity.

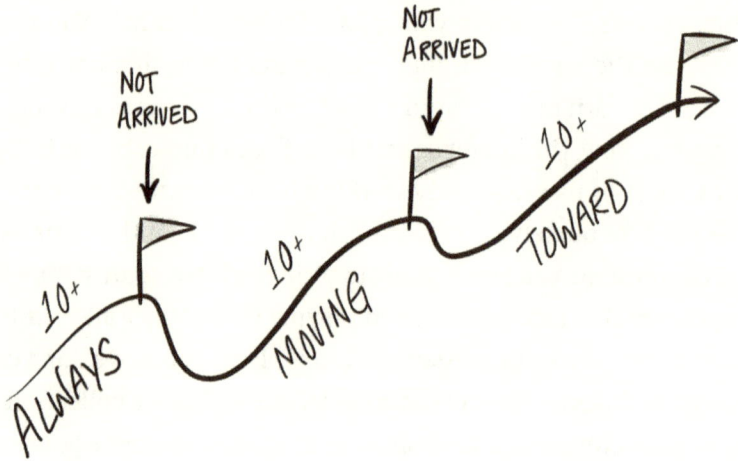

Creating this type of vision isn't hard, but it is often skipped by leaders who think it's *too* far out. If you've ever raised kids, you know that this isn't true—one moment you're tossing them in the air, and the next you're sending them off to college. Time flies! If you aren't clear on what your business will look like in 10+ years, you risk falling short of your best. You might become the business that stays at the same revenue and operational level until you're ready to retire. That may not sound bad, but I know there's so much more for you on the other side.

It Feels Vulnerable

Creating and sharing a long-term vision feels vulnerable, because it is. Putting a bold statement out there about where you see the company in 10+ years exposes you. It opens the door for skepticism, judgment, and even self-doubt. What if the team doesn't buy in? What if external factors change? What if you fall short? These are natural fears, but they cannot be reasons to avoid it altogether. Abraham Lincoln once said, "The best way to predict your future is to create it."

Here's the truth: People are already wondering what the plan is. Whether you spell it out for them or not, they are imagining the future on their own. Some may see growth and opportunity, while others may fear stagnation or uncertainty. Without clear direction, assumptions take over, and those assumptions are rarely aligned. A lack of vision leaves space for confusion, misalignment, and even detachment.

If you don't help your team see the future, they will imagine it for you. And when people create their own narratives, they are often shaped by fear rather than possibility. Instead of a thriving, growing company, they might picture chaos, lack of direction, or even decline. Instead of seeing themselves as part of something meaningful, they may wonder if they have a future with the company at all.

So yes, casting an Always Vision feels vulnerable, but not casting one is riskier. Leaders who embrace this vulnerability and articulate a compelling future give their teams something powerful: clarity, confidence, and a reason to stay engaged in the long run.

CONFUSION	CLARITY
MISALIGNED	CONFIDENCE
DETACHED	ENGAGED

Silence Breeds Ambuguity

One of my first jobs was working with construction foremen, making sure supplies were always ready to keep projects on track. The president of the company was a fiery, quick-tempered guy— one of those bosses you could hear barking orders from the other side of the yard.

Somehow, despite the chaos, he'd managed to build a decent-sized business. But as I got to know the business better, I realized there was 1 big piece missing: a clear vision.

I'd often hear the foremen ask, "What's the plan for expanding? Are we opening a new territory?" I'd just shrug and laugh, because I honestly didn't know. Nobody did. Not even the director of operations seemed to have a clue. The president was tight-lipped and never shared his grand plans—or maybe he didn't have any.

Without a shared vision to rally around, people began to invent their own stories about what the future might hold. It didn't take long for those rumors to breed frustration. Slowly but surely, we watched some of the most experienced employees walk out the door, tired of working in an environment where they felt they were just treading water. That's when it hit me: vision is a necessity for any business—even small ones.

4 Steps to Creating Your Always Vision

The Always Vision is meant to show your leaders and people what's possible. It shouldn't be fluffy, nor unrealistic. It also isn't hard, nor complicated. Here are some steps you can take to create your own.

Step 1: Define Your Revenue Goal

The first step is the easiest for leaders to do: list your revenue goals for 10+ years out. Leaders like this, because there are numbers involved. Occasionally, I see one leader in the group pull out their phone, normally the CFO, and project a number based on their past year's growth percentage.

This is where I stop them and ask the group to be more forward-thinking. I typically encourage them to think about the compounding effects of the things they are doing now. Some of us might have experienced this compounding effect like with process enhancements or hiring key leaders in your business.

You don't see immediate returns, but you have an inclination if it's working well. But years later, you start to see things moving faster, and you can take on more work because you have a system and reliable leaders to help you build your business. So, when you're thinking 10+ years out, it's important to give a number that you almost don't believe to be true. It can also be helpful if you know some other companies in your industry and similar market size—you can use them as a baseline, especially if they have been in business longer.

Step 2: List Out Characteristics, Desires, and Big Goals

Your second step to work toward creating your Always Vision is listing out the characteristics, desires, and future goals you want to see in 10+ years. It's forcing yourself to imagine a decade away. It's hard, but worth it. What we don't imagine, we typically won't work toward or achieve. Here are some examples of this from past engagements we've led:

1. Two new locations serving our clients in the Midwest and East Coast.
2. More owners within the business to help it grow beyond the current owner.
3. Higher-quality products with a lifetime warranty.
4. Be so good and inspiring that people literally write about our company.
5. To be more innovative and create our own proprietary operation's system.
6. Break past the status quo. Be different from our competitors.
7. Be the *go-to* in our region.
8. Create our own software that allows us to service customers better.
9. Give back to our community more with time and money. Write a $100,000 check to entities we believe and trust in.
10. Be a top 100 wholesale distributor in the United States.

Having a target on revenue is important to understand the size, but it's not the end-all. These characteristics, desires, and big goals help describe what these leaders believe will move them toward their revenue goal.

Step 3: Create It

Once you've brainstormed your revenue and identified key characteristics, desires, and goals for your business, the next step is to refine and structure those ideas into an Always Vision. This process involves turning a list of items into a clear, actionable road map that can guide your company. Here's how:

PRIORITIZE AND FOCUS

1. Review the list of characteristics, desires, and goals generated and decide which ones really need to make the list.
2. Identify the elements that are most impactful and align closely with your values and purpose (the next few chapters will touch on this more).
3. Visualize the future in detail. Go beyond broad statements and imagine what success would look like if each aspiration became a reality.

For example, if one is *to be more innovative*, ask, "What specific innovations will define us? How will our customers describe our innovation?"

MAKE IT TANGIBLE AND INSPIRING

Combine your priorities into a single, compelling list that captures the essence of where you want your business to be. Bullets work really well for people like me—no need to create a long-winded statement.

Don't overcomplicate this. Creating an Always Vision shouldn't take long, nor should it bring headache. It should be exciting, so relax and have fun with it. Remember, this is important. It will be the thing that you will look forward to and plan for. Here's what an Always Vision example could look like:

EXAMPLE: 10+ ALWAYS VISION

10+ Revenue Goal: 15 million
Characteristics, Desires, and Big Goals:

- **2 new locations**: Strategically placed in the Midwest and the East Coast, becoming hubs of energy, service, and growth.
- **Higher-quality products**: Every product coming with a lifetime warranty. This inspires us to perfect production and testing.
- **Shared ownership**: Cultivating a culture of ownership by bringing in more owners and partners to help carry the torch beyond the current leadership, creating a future that's built to last.

Step 4: Engage the Team & Plan

1. **Engage and Align the Team.** Share it with your team and gather feedback to ensure alignment and buy-in across your business. Discuss how each department and individual role can contribute to achieving the vision, fostering ownership at every level. This seems daunting at first, but as you keep a rhythm and continue to tweak it as you go, it will feel more natural.

2. **Set Milestones and Create Accountability**. Break the 10+ year vision into some milestones. Discuss and write down how you will know if you are closer to this and

when you roughly expect to get to each milestone. As we move to the Horizon Vision, this will help you *work backwards* from your Always Vision.

By taking these steps, you can transform your Always Vision from a wish list into an inspirational blueprint for growth that is structured and flexible. It becomes a tool to guide decision-making, measure progress, and create a shared future that drives your business forward for the next decade. If you haven't dreamed your future, you'll be *head down*, and before you know it, you'll wonder what happened to the time. To break this down to a more tangible and near future, let's discuss the Horizon Vision.

PART II: THE HORIZON

In nature, the horizon is the point where the land meets the sky. Some days, it's crystal clear. You can see exactly where that line is. Other days, it's hazy, uncertain, and difficult to define. The same applies to the horizon of your business. There will be times when the path forward is obvious, and other times when it requires faith, adaptability, and perseverance.

A Horizon Vision is about inviting others into a tangible future, one that is within sight but still requires time, energy, and strategic execution to fully achieve. This is typically 3 to 5 years out. Many leaders are familiar with setting yearly goals, but goals alone are not enough. Those goals must be driving the company toward a larger destination, a future that the entire team is aligned and working toward.

Think of it like traversing a mountain range:

- Each mountain represents a Horizon Vision: the next major phase in your company's growth.

- The Always Vision is the longer journey: the overarching direction guiding your long-term success.
- To reach the Always Vision, you must climb one mountain on the horizon at a time.

As you hike toward the peak of one mountain, you gain a better view of the next. Even though you know more mountains lie ahead, you must first reach the top of your current mountain to get the best possible perspective on what's next. The journey is never static; it is dynamic, evolving, and full of discovery.

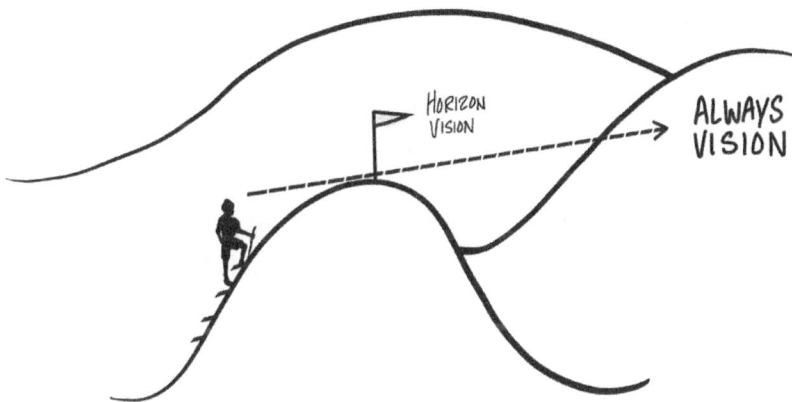

Here are some examples of Horizon Visions:

1. "Expand our product line to accommodate our largest market segment."
2. "Increase our client base by 50%."
3. "Expand our operations to a new territory."
4. "To become the top wholesale distributor in our region."

The last one is from an amazing company, tied directly to their Always Vision. This Horizon Vision drives the team toward the 10+

year journey (Always Vision) of being a top wholesale distributor in the United States (not just in the region). If you're wondering how Horizon Vision is different from goals, I totally get it. The main difference is that goals are more specific with clear time constraints. We want our Horizon Vision to be clear enough to paint a compelling future, but not constrained to a specific date. It needs to be flexible and exciting. The goals leading up to your horizon will be more specific and guide you to achieving it.

3 Steps to Creating Your Horizon Vision

A Horizon Vision helps your company stay focused on the near future while keeping momentum toward the Always Vision. A well-crafted Horizon Vision should be both ambitious and achievable, inspiring your team while remaining practical. Use the following process to define and implement yours effectively.

Step 1: Define Your Next Mountain

Every Horizon Vision is like a mountain in a larger range. It is a significant step forward, yet within reach.

To define yours, ask these questions:

1. Where do we need to be in 3 to 5 years to stay on track with our Always Vision?
2. What goals would significantly move us toward our Horizon Vision?

Let's start with the first question: where do we need to be in 3 to 5 years to stay on track with our Always Vision?

Using prior examples, this shows how the Horizon is leading you toward your Always Vision. I left out some of the details like revenue, characteristics, etc.

- Always Vision: "To become a top 100 wholesale distributor in the United States."
- Horizon Vision: "To become the top wholesale distributor in our region."

This company's 10+ year vision is to be a top 100 wholesale distributor in their industry. But what's on the Horizon? They first must learn how to be the top performer in their region, ensuring people want their service more than others. Who will measure this? They will, and hopefully their customers as well.

More specifically, in their region, their customers will be the judge if they are the top go-to provider. They can measure this by the biggest clients buying from them, by revenue growth, and certainly by how fast they can deliver orders compared to other competitors. Your customers will tell you this one testimonial at a time. When you collect enough evidence, you will have the confidence to say if this is on track or not.

Second question: what goals would significantly move us toward our Horizon Vision?

This is where you will want to take the Horizon Vision and break it down even further. To help come up with some goals, ask, within the next 3 to 5 years, what will help us become the top wholesale distributor in our region? Breaking it down might look like this:

- E-commerce site for our most in-demand products
- A new position of regional manager to oversee sales
- New cloud-based platform for scalability and speed of service
- Faster onboarding and training for new employees

We'll discuss how to turn this into yearly achievable objectives in the Winning Strategy chapter.

EMPTY VISION (ALL TALK, NO WALK)

In college, I worked for a small landscaping business. The owner used to talk endlessly about his grand vision for the company. He wanted multiple locations and to start doing design work. In the beginning, it was genuinely inspiring. His words painted a bright future with young employees growing in their careers and the company gaining more corporate clients. But as I worked on and off for this company during warmer seasons, I started to realize that those rousing speeches were just that—all talk, no walk. No plans followed. No goals were set. No action was taken. The company meetings, once a source of excitement, turned into an eye-rolling routine for everyone involved.

Eventually, people stopped paying attention altogether. They learned that vision without a path to get there is little more than a wish statement—nice to hear, but ultimately empty. This experience taught me that while communicating a vision is essential, pairing it with goals to make it happen is what truly inspires action and earns people's trust.

Step 2: Make It Clear Yet Flexible

Your Horizon Vision should be clear enough for employees to understand and visualize it, but flexible enough to adapt to changing circumstances. A rigid vision can be limiting, while one that is too vague can cause confusion.

- Is the vision specific enough that the team knows what success looks like?
- Can your leaders articulate the vision in their own words, demonstrating true understanding?
- Is the vision adaptable to new opportunities and challenges in your industry or market?

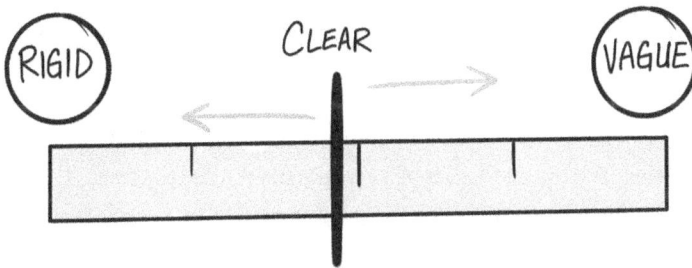

Remember, a well-crafted Horizon Vision doesn't just guide your team. It inspires and empowers them to navigate the unknown with confidence and adaptability.

Step 3: Align and Communicate the Vision

A Horizon Vision should not come from one person alone. It must be shaped collectively by leadership and shared clearly with the entire team. If people can't imagine the outlook of your business, they can't help bring it to life.

To ensure alignment and clarity, ask:

1. Does leadership agree on the Horizon?
2. Can we disagree while committing to it? Even when some people disagree, we should commit to what's best for the company.
3. Has the vision been clearly communicated to employees in a way that motivates them?

4. Can employees see how their role contributes to making it a reality? Your people need to be able to see how they will contribute to the future of your business. This must be practical and relevant to them. One way to do this is to clearly give examples of how each department will help work toward it.

THERE'S ALWAYS ANOTHER MOUNTAIN

A Horizon Vision is not static. It evolves as you gain new perspectives. Once you reach the top of one mountain, you will see the next. That is why the process never truly ends. Instead, it propels your company forward, step by step, toward long-term success.

Creating and communicating a strong Horizon Vision is essential for sustained growth. This ensures teams remain aligned, engaged, and motivated to push forward, even in times of uncertainty.

Without a Horizon Vision, leaders often struggle with:

- **Short-term thinking**: Teams get stuck in daily operations, lacking a clear focus.
- **Misalignment**: Without a shared vision, leaders and teams pull in different directions.
- **Missed opportunities**: Leaders that fail to think ahead may react to change rather than anticipate and leverage it.

When leaders fail to define the next mountain to climb, teams may assume they've already arrived, which leads to stagnation, complacency, and lost momentum. That's why defining your vision is not optional—it's essential.

AWKWARDLY ALIGNED AND READY

Living out your Vision (a combined Always and Horizon Vision) practically can feel awkward in some ways. Like most things, we need to exercise the new muscle and see results. Most of us have probably felt the tension of balancing the future and execution. Often, we will differentiate people from being vision-oriented or operational-focused. Knowing this should equip us to form our teams in diverse ways, but often, we give leadership positions to those who perform based on numbers. We often promote based on how much someone has helped directly contribute to increased revenue.

I don't fault anyone for why this happens, although it is a tension to balance. We often promote and praise employees who drive the biggest results in sales, operations, and finances, directly tied to numerical outcomes. Again, there is nothing wrong with this, but how do we balance this approach? When a team is mostly made up of operational-focused people, there needs to be measures in place to help balance the team with forward-thinking creativity. Visionary or creative people are sometimes not as operationally disciplined and organized. They certainly can be, but it may not be what they naturally gravitate toward. Inviting others who love to imagine a desired future will enable your business to flex a muscle that may have been restrained or weakened at some point. I suggest that you invite people into the room that aren't like you. This doesn't mean that they need a leadership position in your company. They could be temporarily balancing your leaders for areas in your business, like imagining your future. This shouldn't be daunting. It should be exciting, but we have to remember it's a continuum, not an *arrived* mentality. The next part of the 8 to Great is Purpose Driven. This is about aligning your leaders with your vision and driving with purpose, letting it lead the way and give deeper meaning to your work.

TAKE-IT-WITH-YOU NOTE

Vision isn't a fixed point on the map; it's a constantly evolving journey. The most influential leaders understand that it is about continually moving forward as a team.

BONUS: WHEN VISION BECOMES A BLINDFOLD

When a vision is built on outdated assumptions or rigid thinking, it can become a liability rather than a guiding star.

BlackBerry, once the undisputed leader in mobile communication, lost its footing not because it lacked vision, but because it became too narrow and inflexible.

BlackBerry clung to the belief that physical keyboards were one of its competitive edges, until they weren't. As the market shifted toward touchscreens and consumer-centric devices, BlackBerry hesitated. They failed to adapt to a world that was rapidly embracing the app economy and sleek user interfaces. Their vision, once powerful, became a blindfold. They resisted change, and it didn't evolve with the world around them.

There is a critical truth highlighted here: a vision that isn't revisited and refined can create a blindfold. Leadership at Black-Berry was slow to respond to the mobile market, misreading early warning signs and underestimating the impact of new competition. Their delayed response, coupled with a lack of consumer focus and technological innovation, left them scrambling to catch up—unsuccessfully.

To steer clear of Blackberry's same fate, companies must constantly test whether their vision is rooted in truth or nostalgia. As markets evolve, so must the stories we tell ourselves about where we're going and how we'll get there.

WHY VISION?

1. Always Vision pulls you toward a consistent state of becoming better.
2. Horizon Vision is tangible and helps others see what's in the near future.
3. Together, they will help drive your goals and objectives and align them.

CAUTION

1. Don't detach this from your strategy; it's the compass.
2. Don't let it become the *flavor of the month*, dying off quickly.
3. Don't let it become a super vague, unclear thing that no one cares about.

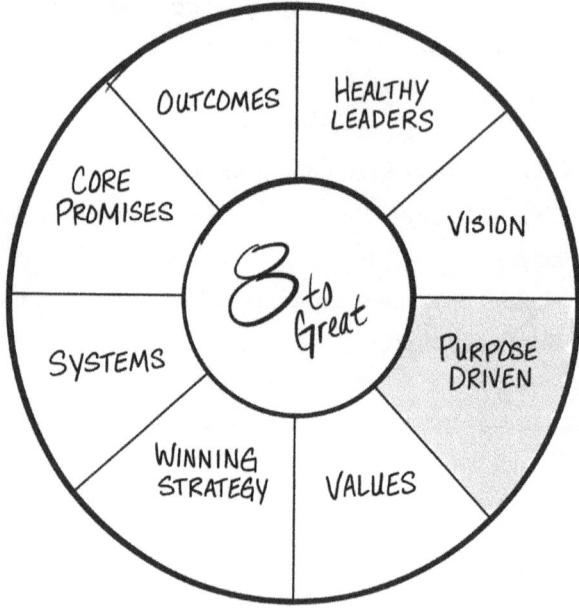

— THREE —

A PURPOSE-DRIVEN BUSINESS

How to Connect
Your Biggest Asset

"The two most important days in your life are the
day you are born and the day you find out why."
—MARK TWAIN

"I HATE IT WHEN SOMEONE tells a story of how this big corporation has grown and made an impact and then tries to relate it to my business." I've heard it a thousand times before. How about I share one of those stories, but then make it so practical that you can't help but take action? As we dive into purpose, let's start by clearing the air. Purpose is not something for the few. It's not rare, nor is it something you need revelation to receive.

Simon Sinek, thought leader and author of *Start with Why*, a book that encompasses how great leaders inspire action, identifies his key word as *inspire*. During a TED Talk, Sinek once described how many great companies like Apple operated in a backward thought pattern. He explained that, regarding their business or life, most people tend to think about the what. What do we do? "We make good computers." Some companies can describe how they do it. How do we make good computers? "They're beautifully designed, simple to use, and user friendly." But Sinek goes on to explain that most companies will not be able to explain *why* they do what they do. He uses Apple as an example, verbalizing how they really think. "Everything we do, we believe in challenging the status quo. We believe in thinking differently. The way we challenge the status quo is by making our products beautifully designed, simple to use, and user-friendly. We just happen to make great computers. Want to buy one?"

When you hear this, it just clicks. Putting an emphasis on the why seems like a no-brainer, but without intentionality, we won't think this way. When we intentionally seek purpose, we will find it. Purpose Driven, within the 8 to Great, is not one thing—it is a collection of reasons you exist and why you contribute to the world around you.

PURPOSE ISN'T FLUFF; IT'S FUEL

Every leader must not only know their purpose but also be able to equip others with the purpose of the company. Many companies have fallen short of integrating their purpose, although I see non-profits and churches doing this better than average, mostly because it's the starting point for them, the cause. On the other hand, most businesses have a much harder time with this concept. We don't blame them, because as Sinek showed us, most people won't think this way.

If every company knew the power of their purpose and learned to amplify it, retention, satisfaction, and focus would skyrocket.

Purpose Driven is a part of the Foundational 4, along with the other 3. Healthy Leadership, Vision, and Values are the lifeblood of a company. We break Purpose Driven into 2 parts: Personal Purpose and Collective Purpose.

In this chapter, you will learn how to discover your purpose and how to communicate it with clarity. I'll help you see how it is directly linked to results, and how it is driven by the motivation and skills of your employees. You'll have the tools to not only put your purpose on paper but to embed it into the very fabric of your business—making it a driving force.

PART I: PERSONAL PURPOSE

Years ago, a particular conversation I was having with a supervisor, we'll call him Bill, gave me some new insight into Personal Purpose. Somehow, we started talking about what got us up in the morning, what kept us going. I remember it, because I thought Bill's response was particularly interesting: "I work for the weekends!" he said with such excitement. "I can't wait to get out and fish with people every chance I get." Since we were at work, I couldn't help myself. I asked Bill what he liked about his job. He said he liked working hard and accomplishing something. Those characteristics, coupled with determination, were just part of his DNA, but it wasn't his love for his work that kept him going. He told me, "I worked hard, and they kept promoting me."

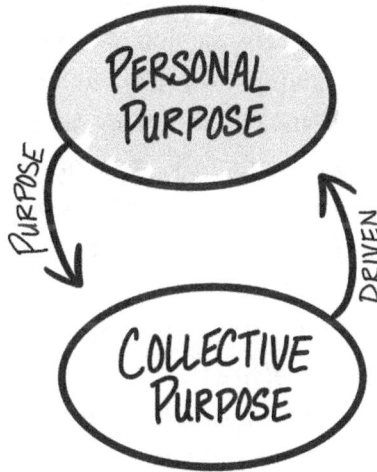

It's not that he didn't like his job. He just had more passion for his hobbies like fishing and being around others while doing it. Maybe you can relate with this, whether it's working for the weekends or being promoted for putting your head down and working hard. Either way, the insight to gain here is that Personal Purpose is different for everyone. For Bill, fishing was connecting to nature and other people—it gave him something to enjoy and work toward. His job was just a conduit to help him fish more, be around people, and have fun on the weekends.

Personal Purpose is the deep-seated drive that shapes an individual's goals, actions, and behavior, reflecting their desire to make meaningful contributions to their own life and the world around them. Take Bill, for example: fishing was a way to connect with others, whether it was teaching his grandson or guiding friends eager to learn. His passion for connecting with people, enjoying nature, and giving back aligned perfectly with this Personal Purpose. When his company's operations manager asked Bill to take clients on a fishing trip, it was more than a professional gesture; it was an opportunity to merge Bill's purpose with his work. That trip left a lasting impression on Bill, giving him a rare chance to align his passion with his career.

Personal Purpose doesn't always appear in such obvious ways. For some, like the incredible project manager I once worked with, purpose was deeply intertwined with his career. This individual, a farmer and military veteran, was relentless in his commitment to excellence. His purpose drove him to lead his team in delivering the largest project in the company's history. While his work ethic was only one facet of his multifaceted purpose, he was also a devoted father, husband, and farmer. It became a defining characteristic of his professional life, seamlessly connecting his personal drive to the company's success. Purpose doesn't just energize individuals. It can align them with the company's goals.

Without purpose, companies risk becoming collections of aimless individuals chasing fleeting thrills or wandering from task to task. When purpose is nurtured and integrated, whether through passion hobbies like Bill's or relentless dedication like the project manager's, it fosters motivation, engagement, and lasting impact for both individuals and businesses.

Purpose Is the Glue That Makes People Stay

Employees who see their Personal Purpose reflected in the company's purpose are more likely to stay with the company long-term and weather the storms with you. This loyalty reduces turnover costs and retains valuable talent, contributing to sustained company performance. It's true that prior generations were known for their loyalty to a company, while more recent generations have adopted a mindset that *moving up the ladder* can quickly be achieved by hopping to the next company. Although this tactic works for some, for others, it just gets them more money in the short-term. You can't always keep people from going, but you can make it incredibly hard.

Leaders must be willing to put in the time of aligning purpose with work. Retention is crucial for maintaining company knowledge and expertise, but I don't need to tell you that. You might have lost an A+ employee at one point, and it might have felt like the end of your business. Without purpose, we have a revolving door, where talent comes and goes with every shiny new offer from others vying to catch their attention. Think back to the project manager, with the great work ethic, in the earlier story. Without the company being able to help him contribute to his work and purpose, he would have ultimately been unsatisfied with the status quo and found other opportunities outside the company. I can understand, if at this point, you're thinking, *How do I align my employee's Personal Purpose with our company?*

That's a fair question. I believe it starts by truly being interested in who they are, and often, helping them articulate their purpose. In many instances, people will have a hard time relaying it for themselves, let alone, sharing it with others.

You Can't Give People Purpose, but You Can Help Them Find It

So, how do we help others find purpose? First, it's important to understand you can't find purpose *for* them, but you can help them on the journey. Most of us have a purpose driving us toward something. As stated earlier, purpose can be a collection of reasons you exist and why you contribute to the world around you.

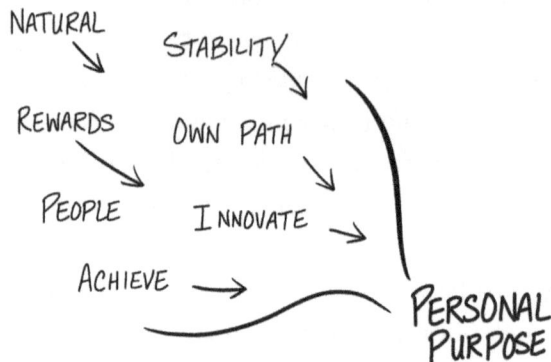

Helping others find their purpose *can* be about creating, but we believe it's more about discovering. Discovering means that purpose might not be as obvious to one as it is to another. When someone doesn't know their purpose, help them shift their focus to others, and they will ultimately find it. Sounds counter intuitive, but it's by affiliation and outward focus that often we too will find our own purpose. Of course, this is the essence of the GIG of a Healthy Leader. Leaders who embrace the GIG will ultimately find purpose and meaning. Sometimes purpose for us does not come easy. One way to help on this journey is by starting with *motivations*.

Motivation Points the Way to Purpose

Motivations are the reasons why people think or act a certain way. There are many motivations that people may have, but with most things, it will likely be multiple variables that reveal purpose, not just one variable or motivation. Think about how many combinations of motivation you might have as you read through these examples and consider how they are tied to your purpose.

- **Growth and Independence**: This is the desire for self-improvement, learning, and mastering new skills. This is often paired with the need for independence and control over one's own actions and decisions. Someone with this motivation will have a natural inclination for a sense of meaning and purpose in their work and/or activities.

- **Rewards or Recognition**: This is the drive toward rewards like financial incentives, bonuses, or other tangible rewards for achieving specific goals. This can also be recognition and appreciation like public acknowledgment and praise for achievements. Other times it can be career advancement, opportunities for promotions, new responsibilities, and professional development.

- **People and Relationships**: This is the drive to feel accepted and part of a group or community. Developing and maintaining meaningful relationships with others and/or working with others toward common goals and experiencing a sense of camaraderie.

- **The Need to Achieve**: This is the drive to set and achieve challenging goals. This could also be the desire to demonstrate skills and capabilities and to be perceived as competent by others. Often, achievement looks like the pursuit of mastering a particular field or subject.

- **Rhythm and Stability**: This is the assurance of stable and continuous employment or routine. The need for a reliable income to support oneself and one's family and/or ensuring physical well-being and a safe working environment.

- **Pave Their Own Path**: This is the desire to influence and guide others. It's the need to have control over one's environment and the outcomes of one's actions. Oftentimes it is paired with holding positions of authority and responsibility within a business.

- **Design and Innovate**: This is the drive to create new ideas, products, and solutions. The desire to express oneself through artistic or creative endeavors and the motivation to tackle complex problems and find effective solutions.

- **Explore and Experience**: This is the desire to explore new ideas, places, or experiences. It's the willingness to take risks and seek out new challenges. This is sometimes expressed in a motivation to travel, explore new cultures, and gain new experiences.

- **The Need to Help**: This is the desire to assist and contribute to the well-being of others. They might have a drive to engage in activities that benefit the community or society at large. Maybe even a motivation to protect and preserve the environment for future generations.

- **The Need for Balance**: The desire to achieve a healthy balance between work and personal life. Often, they need flexible working conditions and schedules. They might want to pursue hobbies, interests, and recreational activities just as much as work. Remember the earlier story of Bill the weekend warrior?

The list could go on. Each of these examples is often paired with the others and creates a unique motivational blend for each specific individual. Motivations are one of the driving forces behind our actions and decisions, acting as the compass that guides us toward fulfillment and meaning. They provide insight into what truly matters to us, revealing the passions, values, and desires that shape our drive. By understanding our motivations, we uncover the *why* behind our efforts, making it easier to align our daily activities with a deeper sense of purpose.

Without this connection, actions can feel aimless, but with it, we are energized, focused, and inspired to pursue meaningful goals. Motivations are a gateway to understanding what is driving someone's thoughts and behavior. When we understand our motivations, we gain insight into what our Personal Purpose is and how we can connect it to our work. Taking this another step further, motivations should be paired with knowing God-given skills and talents. It's as if skills and talents are the compass pointing North, and motivations are the magnetic pull that gives direction to someone's path. It's important to explore how those motivations are aligned with skills and talents.

Your Gifts Are Clues

Pablo Picasso once said, "The meaning of life is to find your gift. The purpose of life is to give it away." As a leader, one of the most rewarding parts of the job is to help others share their gifts. Discovering someone's skills and talents starts with intentional observation, meaningful conversations, and a posture of curiosity. Leaders who take the time to truly know their team by asking thoughtful questions, watching how people naturally solve problems, and noticing where they thrive can uncover the unique abilities each person brings to the table. Tools like strengths assessments, 360° feedback, and even informal "what gives you energy?" discussions can provide clarity and spark deeper self-awareness.

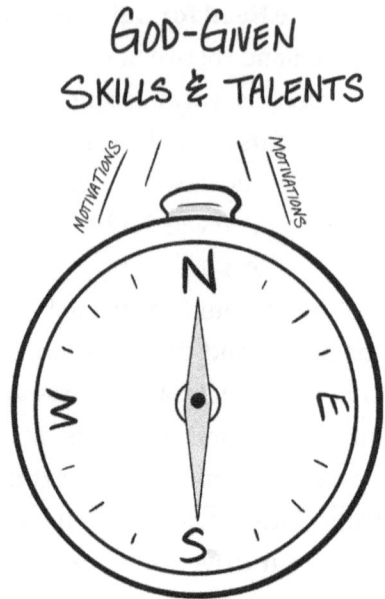

GOD-GIVEN SKILLS & TALENTS

The goal isn't to put people in rigid boxes, but to help them recognize and embrace the gifts they already carry, many of which may not even see in themselves.

Skills and talents are more than just capabilities—they're clues. They reveal what we're uniquely wired to do and often point us toward the impact we're meant to have. When people take time to reflect on what comes naturally to them, what energizes them, and where they excel, they begin to uncover a deeper sense of purpose.

Purpose isn't always found in a dramatic moment of clarity. Often, it's discovered in the consistent use of our gifts to serve others, solve problems, and create value. By stewarding their God-given skills and talents, individuals begin to see not just what they can do, but *why* they're here to do it.

When those skills and talents are paired with internal motivations—what truly drives and excites a person—they create a powerful foundation for aligning personal purpose with organizational purpose. They're not just doing tasks—they're participating in a greater story.

When leaders help their teams discover this alignment, they don't just build stronger businesses—they build cultures where people are activated, empowered, and deeply connected to the work they do.

When It All Clicks: Purpose in Real Life

Once you know yours and other people's motivations and skills and talents, it is easier to link it to purpose. When I was in college, I found purpose in exploring new things like many people, finding what I liked in life, although at the time I didn't realize it was a form of purpose. Fifteen years later, I had been in a privately-held business my whole career, and it was one conversation with a friend that really gave me more insight into my Personal Purpose. As we were sitting together, he asked me about my current job and what I liked. I enjoyed my job a lot. I led many strategic initiatives and helped develop our business across the board with key leaders.

After we talked about those achievements, he asked a question that I'll never forget, "What has motivated you over the years?" It was a hard question, but without much thought I said, "Hard work, people I get to work with, achieving goals..." He didn't let my quick answer go without further prompting. He then asked, "But what's *one* thing that really drives you?" *Boom!* There it was. Until that point, I hadn't realized I had something that drove purpose in my life other than my faith. As mentioned in the beginning of the chapter, often, like nonprofits, our religious backgrounds can be a starting point for our purpose, but there are other reasons why we think and act like we do. Until that point, I had been focused on the outcomes more than a deeper understanding of what was driving me toward those outcomes.

I was motivated by *paving my own path*. For me, that meant I needed autonomy in the company—a way to be an entrepreneur in the workplace. At the time, the company I worked for did just that. They *gave me the keys to the castle*, as they called it. I had built enough trust with them and refined my skills and talents, the president and CFO let me lead important initiatives like leadership development and operational efficiencies. They allowed me to live out one of my purposes in life: creating my own path and developing others along the way. I was able to connect my Personal Purpose with the company purpose and help drive results.

PART II: COLLECTIVE PURPOSE

Collective Purpose is the foundational reason for a company's existence beyond profit. In Chapter 1, we showed that this was the positive (+) direction of the Healthy Leadership Dichotomy. When leaders are moving in the direction of People Focused and Collective Purpose, they are helping the team define their reason for existence within the company. Collective Purpose defines the impact the business seeks to make for people and their community. A strong organizational purpose aligns strategy, operations, and culture toward common goals that transcend financial success. Ultimately, they coincide to contribute to something larger than themselves.

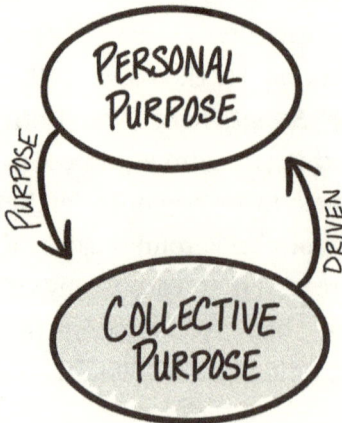

Where Purpose Meets Work

The synergy between personal and business purpose is crucial. When employees find alignment between their purpose and the business, it leads to higher motivation, loyalty, and productivity. This alignment fosters a sense of belonging and meaning, driving success. These words all sound great on paper I know, but it is like anything else in life that's worth pursuing—it takes time and intentionality to make it happen. We have to help our employees find the alignment between Personal and Collective Purpose. But how?

Big Vision, Simple Practice

Google's policy of allowing employees to spend 20% of their time on projects they are passionate about has led to the creation of significant innovations, such as Gmail and Google News. This policy leverages the purposes of employees to drive business innovation. Though most small businesses can't afford this luxury gift, it can become practical for many. For example, one of our clients gave all their employees 3 days a year to help assist any non-profit company they were passionate about. Three days may not seem comparable to Google's 20% of an employee's time, but the impact can be huge when you multiply that by 100+ employees.

From Clocking In to Buying In

When Personal and Collective Purpose align with your vision and goals, employees will be more engaged, motivated, and committed. Why? Because they feel like they're part of something bigger than just endless meetings, grinding away, and replying to emails. They're not just clocking in—they're *buying in*. Though this alignment will never seem perfect, it's worth the effort. We should seek to align all the components—purpose, vision, and goals—as best as possible.

Take Salesforce, for example. This powerhouse CRM software company doesn't just help businesses connect with their customers. It connects its purpose with its business goals in a way that inspires.

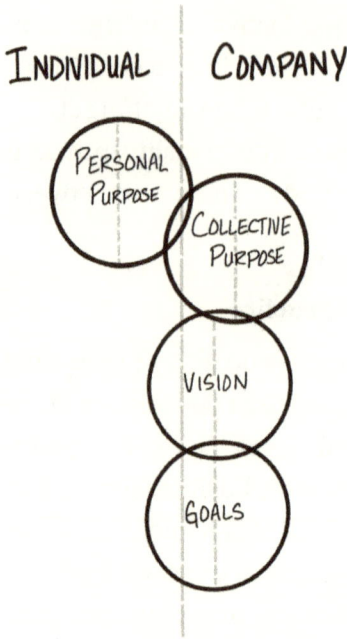

INDIVIDUAL **COMPANY**

PERSONAL PURPOSE

COLLECTIVE PURPOSE

VISION

GOALS

Through its "1-1-1" model, Salesforce donates 1% of its equity, 1% of its employees' time, and 1% of its product to charitable causes. By actively participating in initiatives like environmental sustainability, education, and community development, they're contributing to causes that matter to them personally while simultaneously driving Salesforce's broader purpose. This approach does more than just look good on a corporate brochure. When employees see their values reflected in their company's purpose, they're not just sticking around—they're a part of something bigger. Purpose is the glue that binds personal aspirations with company goals, leading to growth, and impact.

Mission Didn't Die—It Just Needs a Tune-Up

You might be wondering—what happened to the mission? Or maybe you're thinking purpose is just a trendy replacement for the same idea. Mission still matters deeply. It is the *what* and the *how* of your business. It brings clarity to your leaders and direction to your day-to-day operations. Purpose, on the other hand, is the *why*. It is the reason your business exists in the first place. When purpose and mission are aligned, they don't compete. They *fuel* each other. Purpose breathes life and conviction into your mission, while mission turns your purpose into action. For many companies, mission is a catchy statement that lives in a binder instead of the culture. But when it's anchored in a clear and authentic purpose, it becomes more than words; it becomes movement. This story is 1 of many that I've ran into over the years:

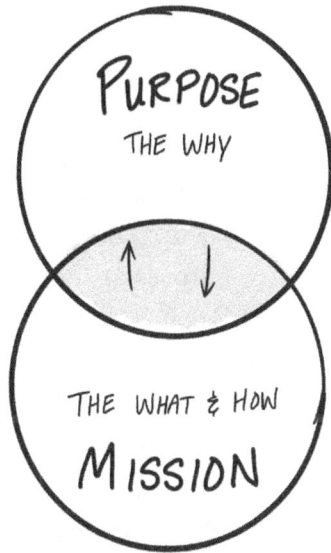

A roofing company we once worked with had hit a wall after years of being in business. They knew they needed something that would unify their team and give deeper meaning to their work. They didn't want a mission statement that sat in a handbook or on a plaque. So, they decided to toss the mission statement and focus on defining their purpose. But as we sat down to work through it, the conversation felt forced. Every attempt at a statement turned into a polished but hollow slogan. "We believe in creating trust by doing great service." It sounded nice, but did it truly capture why they showed up every day?

After an hour of going in circles, I felt the frustration building. So, I switched gears. "Forget the slogans," I said. "Just tell me: why do you work here? Why does your work matter to you?"

At first, silence. It took them a while to just say what they were thinking:

"I love working with great people."

"I like seeing something built with my own hands."

"I want to create something that lasts."

The energy in the room shifted. These weren't corporate buzzwords. They were real, personal reasons. More importantly, they weren't just individual statements; they were connected. These 3 themes—great people, building something tangible, and creating lasting impact—became the foundation of their purpose. In minutes, they had more clarity than they'd found in multiple meetings.

They realized their purpose wasn't about selling roofs—it was about craftsmanship, relationships, and legacy. Once they embraced that, hiring, leadership, and customer experience became easier to share and attract the right people and customers. The best part was their mission statement wasn't trashed; it just needed a few extra bullets to help coincide with their purpose.

View purpose as the vehicle that drives and gives momentum to the mission. The mission is what it aims to achieve. The most important part is that we understand *why* our business exists and what role we collectively play in society. The mission will flow from this in many forms. You can *split hairs* on this, but at the end of the day, the Foundational 4: Healthy Leaders, Vision, Purpose Driven, and Values will be the rock that everything else will be built on. Whether you use the word mission or not, you will naturally be on *the mission*, if you focus building on the Foundational 4.

CLARIFY WHAT'S ALREADY THERE

Your company's purpose already exists, but simplifying or discovering it can be difficult. We've seen companies that have a mission and purpose statement, both relaying very similar things. It was confusing to the leadership team, let alone, the employees. For years, we've seen multiple businesses contemplating whether they should disregard their mission statement, do a purpose statement, only have values, or get rid of it altogether. *Phew*...so many options. The answer is, if what we have is so convoluted that all our employees don't know it and understand how it's connected to their work, we need to simplify it. If you have a mission statement already, don't throw it away. Build on it, add purpose, and make it easy to understand and adopt.

Don't switch things and create a *flavor of the month*. Refine what you have. This is where the rubber meets the road. If you can't *drive with purpose* in your business, you're missing a critical component. This isn't just something you post on your wall or write in a handbook. It's part of your DNA. It's your *why*. Most companies have purpose all around them, made up of the very people within their walls. Just as important, you have purpose baked into what you do as a business. You may not be fighting world hunger, but you exist for a good reason.

PURPOSE ISN'T A SLOGAN—IT'S A PRACTICE

Developing purpose doesn't need to be a long, drawn-out process, but once you have purpose in writing, it becomes a marathon, not a sprint. Your employees are hungry for a purposeful career that connects with their personal being. Invest the time and effort to articulate your purpose.

Do the Work

First, set aside time as leaders. You will need no more than a few hours in most cases. Notice we aren't saying, *purpose statement.* We really believe how you put your purpose to paper depends on your culture. It *could* be a statement, but it could also be a few bullets or a picture—I like those. It should be memorable and help drive passion, collectively.

To ensure that you are hitting all the right components, here is the list of questions you could start with as a leadership team:

- What do we do?
- Who do we help?
- How do we do it?

These questions are designed to help get your mind focused on what you do and how you do it, laying a foundation for deeper reflection. The Healthy Leadership chapter helped clarify these questions, because this kind of clarity is too important *not* to have it on paper.

- What makes you so unique that people would want to repeat it? What would capture the attention of customers?
- Answer these to find some of the differentiators that exist in your business.
- What's the meaning of the work you do? How does this matter to others?

This is where you start to hit on purpose. *Meaning* is a word that is often pushed to the side in business. It can feel squishy, a little too emotional. But like we've discussed in this chapter, purpose is a collection of so many reasons for why you do what you do.

These questions will most likely elicit multiple responses that will help reveal purpose.

Bring It Together

The full process of working through these questions takes time and energy mixed with a little creativity. I don't believe that all companies will have a rigid way to relay their purpose. No matter what it looks like, it's more important that it truly shows purpose and helps your employees connect their purpose to the company. Here are some community business examples that bring all the pieces together:

- **General Contractor**: "We build landmarks that impact the lives and communities we serve." I've heard this repeated by the CEO himself many times. I love how it gives a deeper connection. Employees can see how their jobs directly tie to something bigger. Let's be honest, this statement alone is not going to get people jazzed up. That comes from all the *things* you do afterwards. Like helping a community with their practical needs. This same company took an entire day with half their staff and combed through a small community to help build ramps, fix buildings, repair sidewalks, and a bunch of other things. Employees have seen how they live this out consistently. It's not just about building to them— it's about impact.

- **Commercial Floor Company**: "We grow leaders who deliver best work." This company shows week after week how they develop leaders, not just people who do the work. They want true ownership from employees of what they do. I've repeatedly attended their meetings where they have discussed how far young leaders have come and how they're making an impact. They don't just want people to show up; they want people to *lead* and become relentless craftsmen. They want people who lead their teams, take ownership of their lives, and be an example for their community, friends, and family.

- **Corporate Tax Consulting Firm**: "We help businesses thrive, stay in compliance, and keep their hard-earned money." This shares with employees that their jobs aren't about helping people pay tax but helping them stay in compliance and run their businesses better. They can see how their jobs directly help their customers. The tax world can be dull at times, but we've seen this business throughout the years taking on the best customers like lululemon and Starbucks and helping their employees see their work become more than regulations. It's about keeping these companies around for another 50 or 100 years longer.

Here are a few from some other companies you might know. Because their *reach* is much larger, they have shifted their purpose to be grander, and in some ways, extreme.

- **LinkedIn**: Create economic opportunities for every member of the global workforce.
- **Microsoft**: To help people and businesses throughout the world realize their full potential.
- **Tesla**: To create the most compelling car company of the 21st century by driving the world's transition to electric vehicles.
- **GoDaddy**: We will radically shift the global economy toward small business by empowering people to easily start, confidently grow, and successfully run their own ventures.

For small businesses, it might seem out of the question to have such a grand Collective Purpose, but in reality, each of us has the opportunity to make a large impact in our communities, and beyond. They sometimes call or name these statements differently, but essentially, they are Purpose Driven.

MAKE PURPOSE YOUR OPERATING SYSTEM

Purpose Driven, within the 8 to Great, articulates your fundamental reason for existing, serving as a guiding compass for your strategies, operations, and culture. Here are some ways you can use purpose to drive results and meaning:

- **Strategy**: Aligning strategy with purpose is like turning your company's *why* into its GPS. It ensures every decision and direction leads back to what the business truly stands for.

- **Culture:** This is the beating heart of a purposeful business. Think less *corporate fluff* and more *this is how we roll.* Purpose isn't just what you do; it's why you do it. Culture will continually be formed when the leaders embrace their purpose and don't veer from it.

- **Employees:** It's not just about filling seats—it's about building a team that gets the *why* and is ready to bring it to life. From day 1, onboarding should feel less like a boring orientation and more like an alignment of purpose. Don't stop there. Offer development opportunities that help employees grow in ways that align with your purpose.

- **Customers:** Your purpose should shine in your messaging, creating a narrative that practically taps them on the shoulder. Then, double down by designing customer experiences that reflect the purpose, building loyalty that goes beyond programs or flashy ads. When customers feel connected to your purpose, they're not just buying—they're investing in what you stand for.

- **Innovation:** Use innovation to guide your creative efforts, ensuring every new product or service aligns with the company's purpose. Empower employees to bring forward innovative concepts that advance the purpose. Create an environment where people feel like co-architects of the company's future.

- **Community:** Relationships matter, and aligning your initiatives with purpose ensures your impact isn't just meaningful; it's monumental. Encourage employees to get involved, whether that's volunteering, participating in events. It's easy to skip this one because you don't think you have time, but in reality, it's like anything else. Commit and schedule, or you won't do it.

When Personal and Collective Purpose align, your business will be about more than just the bottom dollar. In this chapter, we've hit on the power of purpose: how to define your own sense of meaning and ignite a shared purpose that unites your entire business. This isn't just about feeling good; it's about driving real results. From empowering employees to tackle passion projects to embedding a deeper why, Purpose Driven success starts with intention and authenticity.

TAKE-IT-WITH-YOU NOTE

Purpose Driven is not 1 thing. It is a collection of reasons you exist and why you contribute to the world around you. Your purpose most likely already exists. Simplifying it can be difficult, but it's worth the journey.

BONUS: MAKE IT COOLLIGAN—AGAIN

There's a really cool retailer in Spain called Coolligan. While I was there, I instantly connected with their purpose. Coolligan exists, in their own words, *to dress the streets with football memories*. They make retro jerseys of clubs and national teams. Now, we love this example because it's on the lighter side. They're not solving world hunger, but they exist to keep football memories alive. If you're reading this and feel a sense of connection, let me stop you there and just say, it's the football that's actually played with your feet, not the American version. But don't let that derail you from the point. Think about if there was a company (maybe there is one) that makes all retro NFL jerseys, and that was their purpose to dress the streets with football memories. That's inspiring, right? We enjoy this company because they provide something that passionate fans will connect with and be proud of. Check out this blurb directly from their website:

THE BEGINNING

Coolligan is the result of a collection of memories, feelings, and emotions. It all happened one afternoon in 2014, while among friends we were remembering the names that had made us live and feel something more than a football match. Those legendary jerseys and unrepeatable teams that the passage of time has become part of our lives.

At Coolligan we want all our customers to have a unique experience. That's why we pay attention to the details of the atmosphere in our stores, from the layout and the furniture to the music. And above all, we pay attention to the personalized attention from our staff.

To date, we have physical stores in Madrid, Malaga, Sevilee, Granada and Barcelona. We also have several corners and multi-brand clients.

Now, think for 1 minute about that question, "What do you do?" It doesn't matter if your answer is more or less important than dressing the streets with football memories. Maybe you supply pipe valves to contractors, or insurance for home and auto. Maybe you build massive buildings, or maybe you sell coffee. No matter what your business does, it has a purpose, and part of your journey will be to not only live your purpose, but to help your employees and customers understand and connect with it. The next chapter flows from purpose and becomes the filter for all decisions, which is values.

WHY PURPOSE DRIVEN?

1. It's not rare, nor does it take revelation to have purpose in your business, but it does have deeper meaning, more than revenue or profits.
2. Without it, we will create a revolving door of employees, ready for the next new shiny offer.
3. Knowing your purpose and integrating it into your business will affect your bottom line and attract the right people.

CAUTION

1. Don't ignore purpose. People want to align their purpose with their work.
2. You can't find purpose for others, so don't try to find it for them.
3. Don't create a catchy purpose statement that you use for marketing.

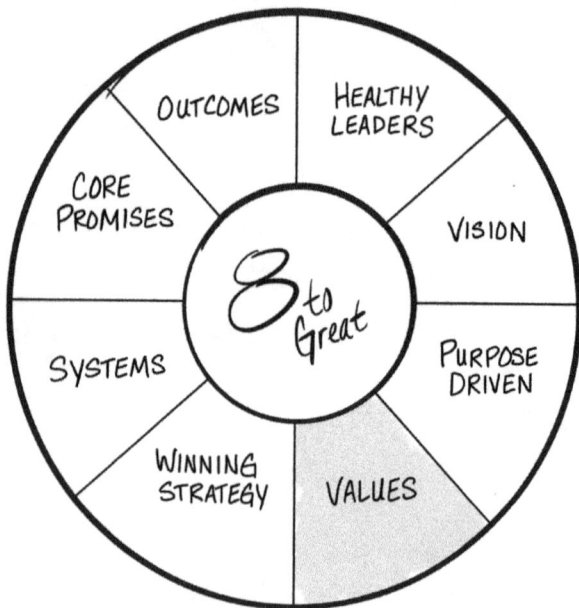

— FOUR —

VALUES-CENTRIC DECISION-MAKING

The Filter That Empowers All

Focus more on your desire than on your doubt,
and the dream will take care of itself.
—MARK TWAIN

AYBE YOU CAN RELATE: The best companies grow because they do great work, and their work becomes more in demand as they prove they can consistently deliver. One company I have in mind doubled their size in just a few years. This successful HVAC company began expanding into new regions across the Midwest. Their leadership team expected the same level of excellence they had built their reputation on to carry into every new territory. They deployed experienced employees to lead each branch—professionals who knew the trade well and had proven themselves.

But within just a few months, customer feedback revealed results were inconsistent. In one region, customers raved about the care and attention they received. In another, complaints trickled in about delays, miscommunications, and a sense of being treated like an afterthought. The difference wasn't in technical skill. It was in how decisions were being made on the ground.

One area manager leaned heavily into logistics, prioritizing speed, efficiency, and job turnover. Another focused on customer experience, going the extra mile to explain options and listen to homeowner concerns. Neither approach was inherently wrong. Both were critical to a healthy operation. But in the absence of clearly defined *values*, each manager defaulted to what they personally believed was most important. And over time, that led to fractured results, frustrated customers, and internal confusion.

When teams don't have a shared set of values to guide their decisions, they start drifting in different directions. Values serve as a compass. They create consistency, empower decentralized decision-making, and give every team member—from the executives to the front lines—the clarity they need to act with confidence and alignment.

VALUES AREN'T JUST WHAT YOU SAY— THEY'RE HOW YOU DECIDE

I was at a business conference years ago, and the speaker mentioned one of his values was to always treat people with respect. You remember the golden rule? Treat others how you would want to be treated. This struck me, in that moment, because I realized how sometimes values can be instilled in us, and yet, we may not behave according to what we value. This is why Values is a part of the Foundational 4 of the 8 to Great. Values are not a marketing slogan that are sold to others. They are deeply ingrained and one of the foundational ways to build a thriving business that doesn't depend on one person to make all the decisions.

In this chapter, we'll discover how many businesses just like yours have used values to obtain the culture and growth they always wanted. I'll share real examples of how values aren't just buzzwords; they are the way you forge something with meaning. You'll discover how to not only leverage your values, but also how to create a system to find and develop people who are extensions of you, becoming one of the ways you scale your business without heartache. By the end of this chapter, you'll be equipped to not only realign your values, if applicable, but also build in ways to scale your business.

THE DECISION FILTER

Values are the filtering system that define the character and culture of your company. They are the funnel for all decisions and help shape our language, behaviors, beliefs, and actions. They are who you are. Roy E. Disney, nephew of Walt Disney and past senior executive of Disney, said, "When your values are clear to you, making decisions becomes easier." Without having centered values and integrating them into your business, you will, inevitably, make decisions based on money, popularity, greed, and who knows what else.

When Values Aren't Just Wall Words

Practical is good, so let's start there with a specific example. DANCER is a polished concrete,

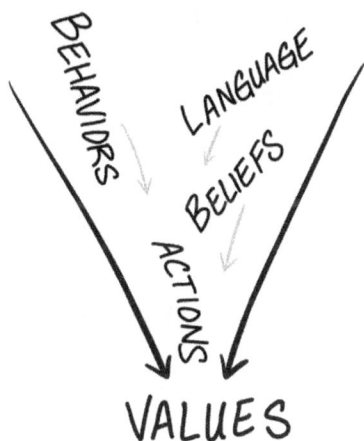

BEHAVIORS LANGUAGE BELIEFS ACTIONS

VALUES

terrazzo, and epoxy flooring company based in Indiana. They do the best work in their region, hands down. DANCER's employees not only know their values, but they are shared each week through a weekly internal newsletter, meetings, and in daily interactions. More importantly, they prove their values have become a guide for all they do in their daily work and interactions.

As you walk into the shop, you're met with huge red letters. Each value is unique to their workplace. And the best part is, they're not just words; they have meaning. We've worked with DANCER for many years, and we see how values have shaped their culture, along with good leadership, vision, and purpose. Their company has been built on the Foundational 4, and they continue to grow at a healthy pace. Each week, the president will capture the team's hard work through an email to the employees and share how values are lived out. I love this for multiple reasons, but I will share 2 in particular.

1. This requires that the leader has a good pulse on the company. You can't discuss how values are lived out unless you are interacting with your people.

2. It informs the rest of the company on how employees have demonstrated values. This helps guide and encourage the right behavior. This is a discipline not every company will embark on, but for DANCER, integrating values in this way, is and will continue to be, a differentiator, setting them apart from the rest.

I would argue it could do the same for your company as well. This discipline of integrating values attracts and retains the best talent willing to put in the hard work. Take a look at their values:

DANCER CORE VALUES

WE ARE...

STRONG AND STEADY
We find a flow in what we take on.
We are known for our hard-work ethic, problem-solving skills, and positive attitude.

NEAT, CLEAN, AND ORGANIZED
A sense of order is not just for good looks.
We believe it supports the flow, drives creativity, and helps deliver the BEST WORK.

MORE THAN ONE
We set aside the pursuit of me, to first serve the mission and the team.

ALWAYS GROWING
We grow by leaning just beyond out security and comfort.
It is our duty to expand upon what we've been given.

THOUGHTFUL COMMUNICATORS
We are intentional with how we speak and listen.
We communicate what is kind, necessary, and true.

Sharing values through a weekly email is a powerful way to reinforce company culture, align teams, and keep the company focused on what truly matters. When leaders consistently communicate values, it reminds employees of the bigger purpose behind their daily work and helps connect individual efforts to the company. A weekly email from the president serves as both inspiration and direction. It's a chance to highlight real-life examples of values in action, recognize employees who embody them, and provide clarity on how these principles guide decision-making. And of course, it's also a time to course-correct, as there are often examples of ways employees did not embody their values. This simple habit keeps values from becoming just words on a wall and turns them into a living, breathing part of the company. Here is a great simple example of how each week, the president at DANCER shares what he sees:

The core values you'll hear in our business weren't picked from a book. They were forged by real people doing realy work over the years. These values aren't just something to follow when it's easy. CORE means we hold to them even when it's hard.

Everyone says they believe in the same things. **However, actions and sacrifices separate the talkers from the builders**. Here are some of the people who brought these values to fruition.

Strong and Steady: Joel is a rock. He is consistent, steady, finding solutions, and keeping a good attitude no matter what's thrown at him.

Neat, Clean, and Organized: Ben D keeps out show clean, trucks stocked, and doesn't walk past a problem. Whether it's his trash or not, he picks it up because he's got the mindset of a true caretaker.

More Than One: My wife is a powerhouse. She's played the long game with wise decisions, sacrifice, and generosity. So many others would have said, "*Stop, that's enough*." But she keeps supporting our family and business.

Always Growing: Ben R had a lot of potential. The "old Ben" made excuses and looked for shortcuts. The Ben you see today grew into a strategic-thinking craftsman because he chose to keep growing when it got uncomfortable.

Thoughtful Communicator: Jake leads with clarity and respect. He listens before speaking. Nothing is a reaction. Everything he says is kind, necessary, and genuine. When he says something will get done, it gets done.

This is who we are. This is what we're building.

DO YOUR VALUES SOUND LIKE YOU— OR A BROCHURE?

Similar to vision and purpose, values are something that need to be intentional in order to identify what speaks to your company. If your company already has stated values, don't stop reading, thinking that the job is done. This will also serve as a gut check and good reflection. Many companies will blare their values without going through the proper channels to ensure they are adopted and a part of their culture. When companies adopt values that speak to their culture, people will see it as a genuine approach and will be more likely to adopt them as their own.

First, we must use language that's fitting to our people. Whether that's humor, deadly competitiveness, a serious approach, being extremely accurate, or whatever else captures who you are. Take a look at a company who has a unique set of values: Airbnb. These values come straight from their website:

Champion the Mission
We're united in partnership with our community to create connection, which enables belonging.

Be a Host
We're caring, open, and encouraging to everyone we work with.

Embrace the Adventure
We're driven by open curiosity, hopeful resilience, and the belief that every person can grow.

Be a Cereal Entrepreneur
We're determined and creative in transforming our bold ambitions into reality.

Just for a second, think about how these 4 values represent Airbnb and are tailored with their own language. A friend shared a story with me about his experience with Airbnb. He was on the phone with one of their customer reps, explaining that they weren't able to get a refund from their host. He explained that their flight had been canceled at the last minute and their airline couldn't find them another flight to the location. My friend was fired up, especially since it was 7 days in a beach condo that wasn't being refunded.

As he explained the situation to the Airbnb representative, the person on the other line continuously reiterated their understanding by saying, "If I were in your shoes, I would feel the same way." By the end of the call, Airbnb actually helped them get another stay through the original host. Now, I don't want to advertise that they will be able to help everyone in this way, but because of the unique variables, there was something they could do. The representative didn't ask my friend to hold 7 times while he did the cliche car lot manager negotiation thing, nor did he give excuses of *that's just how the cookie crumbles*.

If you've experienced bad customer service (and haven't we all?), I'm sure you can relate. This Airbnb representative certainly had the characteristics of an entrepreneur and a host. When running your business, you understand to put yourself in the customer's shoes in order to relate and find win-win solutions, but it's hard in the moment. Maybe this representative was just empathetic, or possibly, they were embracing one of the values that Airbnb had permeated into their culture. In this example, we see the value, "Be a host," was not only to be embraced by property owners renting their space to others, but it was meant to be lived out by every employee. "It takes one to know one" is a statement that may take you back to middle school, but in the business world, it certainly does help if people can put themselves in other's shoes like in this story. This is why values are a part of the Foundational 4; they become the guiding lanes of your company.

The Discipline of the Obvious

Years ago, I had the privilege to listen to Horst Schulze, who successfully led Ritz-Carlton Hotels for many years. He didn't state any of their values, but he used the same principles under the title of a mantra. I understand that a mantra is not values, but how they are used are closely related—so stick with me. Horst shared in his German accent, that all his employees would carry a card in their pocket that relayed how they would treat customers. It was a gentle reminder that one of their values was the world-class way they treated customers. He stated that employees would read it each day before the shift began.

Just imagine if we had that kind of discipline in our businesses! Now, I've never been to a Ritz-Carlton, but I know that other hotels have used their practices as a guide for how they train and teach employees. Simply put, other businesses and hotels saw how important it was to keep values centered and focused every day. They copied Ritz-Carlton, because they saw the output of this discipline.

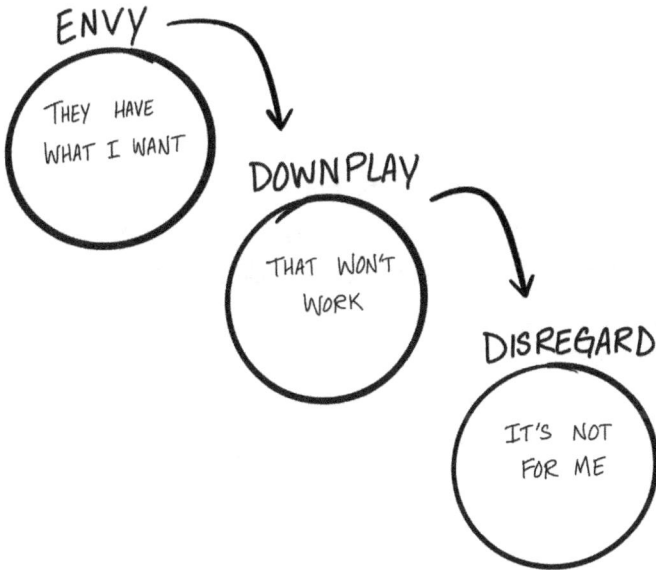

Sometimes we think it is just too simple: it won't work—remember Envy Downplay? We shy away from believing that posting some values on a wall or some cards in a pocket could actually help create a mindset for your employees. Maybe we think, *That won't work. The employees won't value what I (president) value. They won't care as much.* The truth is, some won't care, but using the values in all facets of your company will consistently create a mindset for your employees to choose for themselves. Ultimately, creating the culture you want by embedding them into everything, will lead employees to see your values and adopt them, or get out of Dodge.

Here's the scenario: values are set. They are well communicated, and they are talked about often by all leaders. Employees will have to make a decision if they value the same thing or not. If not, they will work themselves out of your business, or you will start to find them and show them the door. Either way, values become your guiding path for big decisions like who can be a part of your company.

3 BUCKETS

There are 3 categories or *buckets* of values that help us define what it means to be values-centric. The buckets help us understand how our values shape our thoughts, beliefs, and actions. Without this insight, we risk spouting off values that make employees roll their eyes. Ensuring our values are clearly defined but also genuinely embraced by everyone is crucial. After all, we want to walk the walk, not just talk the talk. Don't worry if you already have stated values for your company. I have worked with plenty of leaders who have adjusted their wording to help bring more clarity and tailor it to their culture. Maybe this will help you going forward.

ADOPTED   NATURAL   WORKING

Adopted Values

Adopted values are like hand-me-downs from our past or current environments. We pick these up based on what's worked elsewhere or what's trending in the business world. For example, we might embrace innovation or customer-centricity because, hey, if it worked for others, why not us? This can be dangerous if you adopt the values but don't embrace them. This bucket is filled to the brim with all the ones we've *collected* through the years, starting with our childhood. Remember all the values your family and friends taught you? Whether you agreed at the time or not, you collected them and took them with you. We then need to decide if we truly adopt and embrace them or let them go. Since our businesses are made of people from all sorts of backgrounds, it's important not to adopt values based on one person or experience, but as a whole.

Natural Values

Natural values are the ones that just flow out of our daily grind. These values are shaped by the collective behaviors and vibes of everyone in the business. Think of it like a strong aroma of teamwork and collaboration wafting through the office, simply because our team rocks at supporting each other and working together. This is extremely important to pay attention to and capture. It's also why we all must be very careful in who we allow on our teams. Our people form our natural values. The natural bucket is still being filled one day at a time, and eventually, we'll have collected enough evidence to know which ones are natural and not just adopted. These values take discipline to maintain as growth continues in your business. As you cycle through different phases of growth, it might be tempting to gravitate toward what's worked for others.

I see many businesses transforming their culture as they grow, but not even realizing how they altered who they were. Different growth cycles can erode Natural Values. It's up to leadership to ensure that it is an intentional *let go* or *keep*, rather than an unintentional slipping without realizing it. Keeping track of this requires you first have your values integrated into the fabric of your business, reading them out loud like Ritz-Carlton, and ensuring you are using them for decisions.

The Values We're Still Becoming

Working Toward Values are our wish list items. These are the values we dream about but haven't quite nailed yet. It's like aspiring to be the yoga master when you can barely touch your toes. We identify these values to set goals and create action plans, aiming for ideals like sustainability, innovation, and diverse thinking. With a bit of effort and commitment, we can turn these values into reality, one at a time. This bucket is like one drop at a time, voting our way to filling it and solidifying the values and behavior, working toward what we wish to become. Working Toward Values take the leadership's attention, and discussions with all the teams across your company.

Becoming the Business You Want to Be

We worked with a company that desired the value of clean and organized, but it was evident that it didn't exist in their current culture. The leadership team agreed that it was needed, but the employees had not embraced it as a value. With coffee cups on the stairs after each day, leftover supplies on the floor, and employees not putting back tools, they know they needed some help. But the leaders did not relay this value with the employees, so how could they integrate what was not communicated? If we say we want something without first writing it down and communicating it, then we are just wishing. That's why this third bucket is called Working Toward, not Wishing For.

As practical as this may sound, often, it's hard for leaders to transparently say, "We are working on this, but clean and organized isn't quite a value. Here are some ways we think we could start to move toward making it a value..." When leaders start with this level of transparency, they can truly start working toward the desired value. They can start with a list of what to work on, then share some examples of what the desired state should look like before the company would name it as a value. Why is this hard for leaders to do? There are probably many reasons, but one in particular is vulnerability. It takes vulnerability to say, "We aren't there yet." Then, to collectively try to work toward it. Another reason might be fear of not being able to achieve it. Either way, it feels vulnerable in many instances.

This is hard because we're talking about behavior, not just a tangible operational goal to achieve. Behavior is always hard and feels more vulnerable to work toward, not to mention it takes consistency to actually progress in the desired direction. It's simple, but hard to put your neck on the line. Maybe you think, *Our team will never embrace this*, or, *What if they just can't do it?* What I've witnessed is that your employees can see if it's a genuine approach to improve the company, and most likely, they already know it's needed.

That same company took one step at a time. For 3 months straight, we discussed how coffee cups didn't belong on the stairs and should be taken up to the break room and put in the dishwasher. Week after week, we saw improvement happening one cup at a time. After small steps like that, we started talking about clean-up days for leftover supplies. That value got closer and closer to reality. Obviously, this value was about more than coffee cups. It was a part of a larger value to become a clean and organized company. Take one step at a time and be disciplined at discussing each week until you see change happening. This will propel you toward becoming it, not wishing it were true. Whether you're a large company with multiple locations or small with one location, moving toward a desired value is focusing on what part of the company needs the guidance to work toward that value. Focusing on the parts of the company that need shoring up will eventually help your employees create alignment. This takes consistency and communication from all of your leaders.

LEAVE YOUR VALUE FINGERPRINT ON EVERYTHING

Elvis Presley once wisely said, "Values are like fingerprints. Nobody's are the same, but you leave 'em all over everything you do."

I bet that might be the first Elvis quote in a business book. Values are something to be built on. They're used for filtering decisions and people for your company. Your value fingerprints should be left on everything you do. Here are some of the big areas to integrate your values:

- **Hiring and Onboarding**: Hiring is like trying out for a sports team. You want the right athletes who can play their roles well and align with your culture. We want to look for people who not only have the skills but also resonate with your values. If collaboration is a value, you might want to avoid the ones who prefer running alone. During interviews, toss in some quirky efforts that reveal their true character by asking open-ended scenario-based questions. Then have them share their values and how they would respond. Onboarding new employees is like hosting a welcome party. You want them to feel at home and understand the house rules (values) from the get-go. Skip the boring presentations and have leaders share stories of how they have integrated company values throughout their journey.

- **Strategy**: When it comes to strategic decisions, think of your values as the secret sauce that gives your business its unique flavor. Whether you're planning to expand to a new market, launch a groundbreaking product, or simply create a new training curriculum, let your values guide you. If innovation is a value, don't settle for the same old strategies. Spice things up wisely. Try new approaches, experiment, and maybe even throw in one of those *standing meetings* to get ideas flowing. Strategic decisions should align with your values to keep everyone on the same page and prevent any *What were they thinking?* moments.

- **Operational or Tactical Decisions**: Operational or tactical decisions are the day-to-day moves that keep your business running like a well-oiled machine. Your values should be the beat you're moving to. If efficiency is a value, streamline processes and cut the fluff. If sustainability is your jam, make eco-friendly choices in your operations. When everyone understands the rhythm of your values, even mundane tasks can feel part of a larger picture. Plus, it makes those daily meetings more of a synchronized routine instead of a countdown.

- **Letting Go**: Firing people is never fun, but sometimes it's necessary to stay on track and aligned. When values are at the heart of your company, it's easier to make these tough decisions. If someone's actions are out of sync with your values, it's like having a cellist playing death metal at a classical concert. Address issues early with a focus on your values. If things don't improve, it's time for a respectful but firm exit.

Remember, it's about maintaining a cohesive, values-centric culture, not just filling seats. Incorporating values into every facet of your business keeps the spirit alive and kicking, ensuring that everyone is not just part of the company, but aligned, moving in the same direction. This is why I created the Escalator Model.

ESCALATOR MODEL

The Escalator Model is a way to understand how to build and replicate value-based people in your business. Building on values to find the right people involves an approach that includes finding, developing, empowering, multiplying, and filtering through values repeatedly. Once you get a system rolling, you can then build and replicate it, like an escalator revolving stairs one step at a time. Here's how you can infuse each step with your values to ensure you're attracting and retaining the best people for your business.

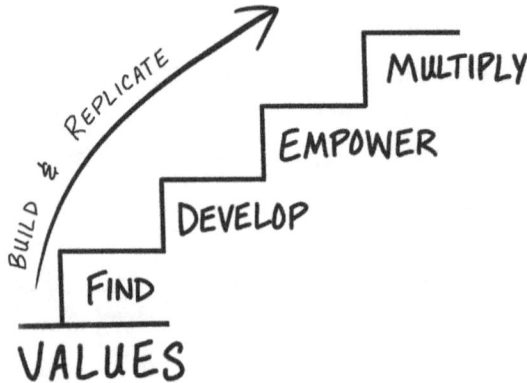

1. **Find**: Finding the right people starts with casting a wide net but with a clear bait—your company values. When advertising job openings, highlight your values prominently. Are you big on innovation? Make sure your job descriptions reflect a culture of creativity and forward-thinking. This way, you attract candidates who not only have the skills but also resonate with your ethos.

2. **Develop**: Once you've found aligned people, develop their potential in line with your values. Create training programs that not only teach job-specific skills but also reinforce your values. If *Grit* is a cornerstone value, incorporate past hardships and real-world scenarios that employees might face. Provide continuous learning opportunities that allow employees to grow both professionally and personally. Encourage mentorship programs where seasoned employees embodying your values can guide others.

3. **Empower**: Empowering employees means giving them the autonomy and tools they need to live out your values in their daily work. Trust is a key component here. Demonstrate this by giving employees the freedom to make decisions within their roles. Encourage innovation by allowing employees to experiment and take calculated risks. Calculated is the key word here. As we discussed in Chapter 1, this requires guidance. Recognize and celebrate when employees demonstrate your values, whether it's through awards, shout-outs in meetings, or other forms of appreciation. This not only motivates individuals but also sets a clear example for others to follow.

4. **Multiply**: To multiply your talent, values must run deep throughout your business, ensuring that they are consistently communicated and reinforced. This can be done through regular training sessions, workshops, and team-building activities centered around your values. Create a culture where employees are encouraged to share stories and examples of values in action. For instance, a company newsletter/email could feature values like the DANCER example. This creates a ripple effect, ensuring that your values are continuously propagated and ingrained in the company culture.

5. **Filter**: Finally, filtering ensures that everyone in your company remains aligned with your values. Regular performance coaching should include an assessment of how well employees embody the company values. If someone is consistently out of step with your values, it's important to address this early. Small problems will inevitably accumulate into big ones. Offer additional training or

coaching to help them become aligned. Maintaining a strong values-centric culture sometimes means making tough decisions, but it's crucial for the overall health and integrity of your business.

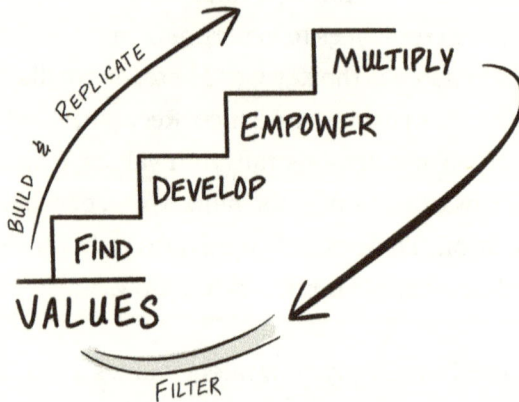

By integrating your values into every step—from finding to filtering—it ensures that every hire, development plan, and performance coaching is not just about skills and output, but also about being unified.

BUZZWORDS SUCK

If you're still thinking after reading this chapter that values are buzzwords and those suck, you're right! If that is all values are to a business, then yes, they should just throw values away. But what if some businesses have been doing it wrong? What if they have given values a bad name because they aren't an authentic combination of the Adopted, Natural, and Working Toward Values? What if they weren't actually upholding them, or they were pursuing things without filtering everything through them?

If that's true, then yes, they have become just buzzwords, but if we pursue running a business with true integrity with our values, what will happen? Okay, enough with the *what-ifs*. If a company has values like integrity, honesty, diversity, blah blah blah, they probably have very little intentionality. These are buzzwords, no doubt. It's easy to say these broad terms and not integrate them into your business.

One time, I was doing a workshop at a company, and I started out by asking their employees to state the company's values. Now, I'll pause to say that these were plastered on their website and also on the entrance of their glass wall. Out of 60ish people, not one spoke up right away. Not even the head HR person. I then said, "You passed them on the way here." Still, crickets. So, I said, "They're pretty common words..." Finally, 2 or 3 said, "Integrity," while another said, "Respect!"

I couldn't help but laugh. All it took was me saying that they were pretty common words, and people started to state the company's values. It wasn't long before leadership thought about making their values a bit more tailored to their business. Buzzwords suck, so don't do it.

Values are the filtering system that define the character and culture of your company. Values are the funnel for all decisions, and they help shape our language, behaviors, beliefs, and actions. Values are who you are, shown through actions and behaviors. With them, clarity replaces confusion and momentum replaces friction. Becoming a values-centric business is a commitment. When your team embodies your values, you unlock next-level alignment, deeper engagement, and a culture that attracts and keeps the right people around. The right people will show up, and stay, because they believe in what you stand for. Examine your Adopted, Natural, and Working Toward Values, and weave them into every part of your business, from hiring and strategy to customer experience. Above all, live them. Your people are watching.

TAKE-IT-WITH-YOU NOTE

It's simple, but hard to work toward values. But if your employees can see it's a genuine approach to improving the company, and most likely, they already know it's needed, they will go on that journey with you.

As we move to the Operational 4 of the 8 to Great, think about the Foundational 4. How do you build on them daily? Where do you see the evidence in your business?

BONUS: WHY NOT *CORE* VALUES?

Core values are often seen as the unshakable foundation of a business, intended to guide behavior, shape culture, and influence every major decision. But in practice, many businesses choose values that sound good on paper rather than reflect how the company actually operates. When values become aspirational rather than operational, they can quietly cause more harm than good. If they're not lived out daily, they become a source of confusion or even cynicism, undermining trust rather than building it.

We once worked with a company whose founding value was *family first*. It made perfect sense in their early days, which started by a tight-knit team with deep local roots. Their culture thrived on familiarity and personal connection. But as the company grew and the Founder stepped away, things began to change. They started hiring from outside the region, expanding into new markets, and setting their sights on a national presence. Internally, though, there was tension. New leaders didn't feel part of the original *family*, and some employees felt like outsiders, unsure how to live out a value that no longer reflected their day-to-day experience. The leadership team had to make a tough but honest call: either course correct and rebuild the culture around that value, or redefine what truly mattered now. They chose the latter, shifting their core value from *family* to *belonging*: an inclusive, future-focused principle that still honored the heart behind the original intent, but better aligned with where the company was headed. Their intentionality to evolve with their values helped them align as a company as they pursued new ventures.

That's why values should be treated with the same discipline as strategy: regularly revisited, stress-tested, and refined. *Core* implies permanence, but if a value no longer reflects how your company thinks, acts, or aspires to grow, it might not be core anymore. That's not failure—it's maturity.

WHY VALUES?

1. Values take intentionality. They keep us formed and aligned.
2. They are the filtering system for all decisions in your company, including hiring and firing.
3. The Escalator Model shows how it's a continued process, not a one and done.

CAUTION

1. Ensure you know if they are Adopted, Natural, or Working Toward Values.
2. If you post them somewhere, ensure they mean something and talk about them.
3. Don't let them become buzzwords that no one cares about.

GET YOUR HEAD ABOVE WATER.

—NATE BARGATZE

This blank page is for reflection purposes and is brought to my attention as a needed break by Nate Bargatze, "The nicest guy in comedy."

As he once stated about books, "...too many words and they just keep going and going." We all need to get our head above water sometimes. We put in this blank page here for those who need a break.

OPERATIONAL 4

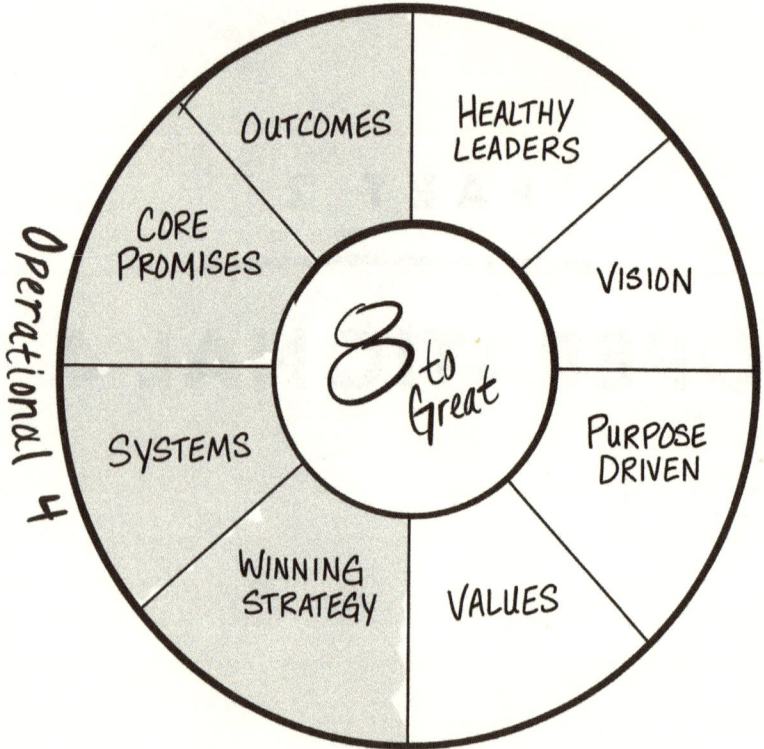

Operational 4

OUTCOMES
HEALTHY LEADERS
CORE PROMISES
VISION
8 to Great
SYSTEMS
PURPOSE DRIVEN
WINNING STRATEGY
VALUES

The first 4 components: Healthy Leadership, Vision, Purpose Driven, and Values are the *Foundational 4*. As we discussed, to integrate these 4 components well, you first must believe that your company is a breathing live organism that is consistently in need like any human being. Starving the business of these first 4 will inevitably choke the rest of the company.

The next set is the *Operational 4*: Winning Strategy, Systems, Core Promises, and Outcomes. Both the Foundational and the Operational 4 make up your culture. The next 4 chapters will show how you build on the Foundational 4 with the Operational 4 of the 8 to Great. **Become what you cultivate.**

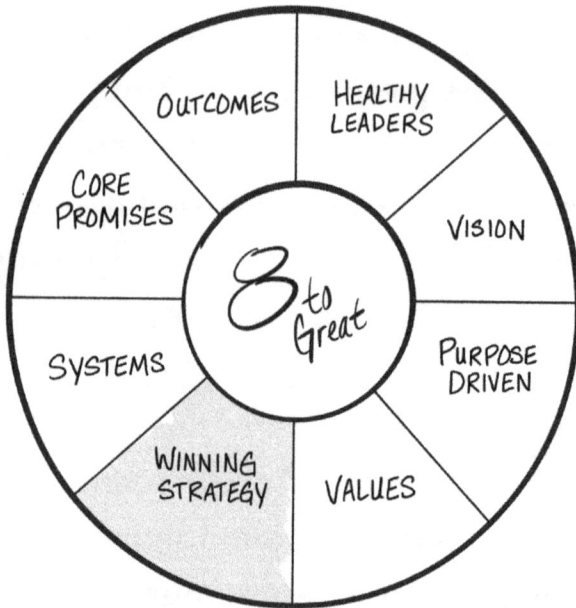

OUTCOMES

HEALTHY LEADERS

CORE PROMISES

VISION

SYSTEMS

8 to Great

PURPOSE DRIVEN

WINNING STRATEGY

VALUES

FIVE

DEVELOP A WINNING STRATEGY

The Process *Is* Your Strategy

> Whenever you find yourself on the side
> of the majority, it is time to pause and reflect.
> **—MARK TWAIN**

N AUGUST 1944, Paris was finally liberated from brutal Nazi occupation. They were freed by the Allied forces and the French Resistance, emerging from the war with its aesthetic beauty and essence largely intact. Declaring Paris an open city, while bitter and painful, was a choice, one that came with unknown outcomes prior to making the strategic decision.

In 1940, France faced a time of immense uncertainty as the relentless advance of German Nazi forces drew closer to the heart of the nation. The French military had already suffered devastating losses, with many soldiers taken prisoner, and morale was deeply shaken. The leadership faced a dire dilemma: defend Paris and risk its destruction or make a painful decision to spare the city from becoming a battlefield.

The memories of the First World War, during which Paris had narrowly escaped devastation, loomed heavily in their minds. As the German forces approached, in June of 1940, the French government declared Paris an *open city*. This meant no military defense would be mounted, and all armed forces were withdrawn to avoid urban combat. The decision, though agonizing, was made to preserve the city's architectural and cultural heritage, as well as to prevent the civilian casualties that a battle within Paris would have surely caused. German troops entered Paris, finding it eerily quiet and unscathed. This act of surrender was not without its controversies. Some viewed it as a pragmatic and humane decision, while others saw it as a concession of defeat.

For the next 3 years, France would endure Nazi occupation. Throughout this dark period, the French spirit was still alive. In 1944, France had gained control of the city once again upon the defeat of the Nazi army. This historical moment offers a profound lesson about leadership, strategy, and decision-making. Imagine being in the room with French leaders that day as they faced the unbearable weight of their choice. It wasn't a decision anyone wanted to make, and it likely sparked deep disagreement and debate.

Strategy is about making real decisions that have outcomes. Let's get into that.

STRATEGY IS THE COURAGE TO CHOOSE

In business, as in life, decisions often carry unknown outcomes. Leaders are forced to weigh incomplete information, conflicting priorities, and the consequences of their choices. Like the French leaders, we sometimes face the need to make decisions we'd rather avoid, knowing the future remains uncertain. Strategy, much like wartime leadership, involves navigating the unknown and making the best-informed choices for the greater good. For some businesses, these choices require not taking on too much work that inevitably leads to destruction. For others, it is putting up a fight against your competitor and creating a new product. While not every decision will lead to clear victories, the act of choosing—of moving forward despite uncertainty—is what defines us.

Strategy is often used in business to sound smart or important. It's like saying, "According to research..." If all else fails, just say, "Our strategy is..." and people will most likely think you have a decent plan. We've observed a lot of businesses call something strategy, when really it was a *to-do* list or something that made them feel good. Benjamin Franklin said, "Success is the residue of planning." Planning requires us to make the best predictions with the best information we have available.

> *Winning Strategy is the art of planning,*
> *executing, and moving toward your vision*
> *with the right information and people.*

This is a culmination of integrating the Foundational 4, planning the future, and developing the discipline of action to get results. It is the process of planning internally, just as much as externally. It's the weighted balance of people and process and ensuring your products and services are dialed in to the best of your ability. People refers to your employees and customers, and processes include everything from business development to customer satisfaction.

In this chapter, you will walk away with a detailed process to form your Winning Strategy. Strategy is the backbone of any operation and serves as the action to your vision. There's no one answer for your business; it's formed in a process of choices. You'll learn insightful ways to set aside the whirlwind tasks and align your team and company to work toward lasting results.

INERTIA OR OVERTAXING

When we start working with companies on their Winning Strategy, I often see leaders wanting to *bite off more than they can chew*, or what we call overtaxing. This can probably be explained for many reasons, like ambition, pride, unrealistic foresight, lack of understanding, and much more. It's not uncommon to hear a 3-year plan being rolled into 1 year. We often have a problem with consuming more than we can handle. Our eyes are bigger than our stomachs, and many of us could agree that doing too much will often lead to apathy. We might think it's noble, but it won't be long before we crash, burn out, and nothing gets done.

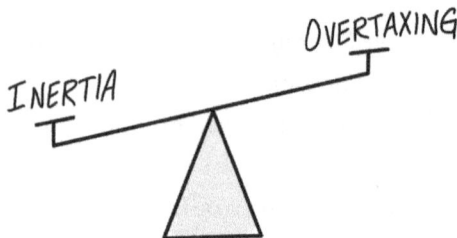

Or maybe on the flip side, its inertia, paralyzed by the fear of what will happen. We might fear the unknown and decide not to move until we have *all* the information. None of us will ever have *all* the information. The unknown of what's on the other side of your choices is an abyss. It will suck you in and never let you out. It's your choice.

Balancing these 2 extremes means that we need to focus, create stretching goals, and minimize the risk we can foresee. Much like the story of Paris, we can choose to take on what we know will inevitably destroy us, or we can face reality and make strategic decisions that hopefully sets us up for success when the time is ready. Or maybe, if nothing else, just remember what Mike Tyson shared once, "Everyone has a plan until they get punched in the face." A gentle reminder that planning is just a piece of it all. How we react is key. While the concept of strategy may seem daunting, we can break it down into a structured, logical process.

4 PARTS OF THE WINNING STRATEGY

To better understand strategic planning and execution, let's break it down:

1. **The Now, Current State**: Thoroughly assessing your business's present reality, including feedback from customers, employees, and market trends.
2. **Desired Future**: Revisiting your compelling vision—both the long-term Always Vision and the nearer-term Horizon Vision—to ensure it remains clear, relevant, and motivating.
3. **The Path Forward**: Outlining the specific objectives, initiatives, and resources needed to bridge the gap between your current state and your vision.
4. **Effective Conveyance**: Communicating the strategy in a way that engages and aligns your entire team around the plan.

Just note, these are essential to the Winning Strategy, but there's something that is often overlooked, which is the Foundational 4: Healthy Leadership, Vision, Purpose Driven, and Values. They're all key to integrate into your strategy. Check out this sketch that shows how they're all connected. It looks like a fine balance of flower power and strategy.

Strategy is an ongoing process. The process itself reveals your strategy, which evolves over time and is fueled by the most critical resource in your company: your people. It's *not* the magical plan that moves the needle but the individuals behind it.

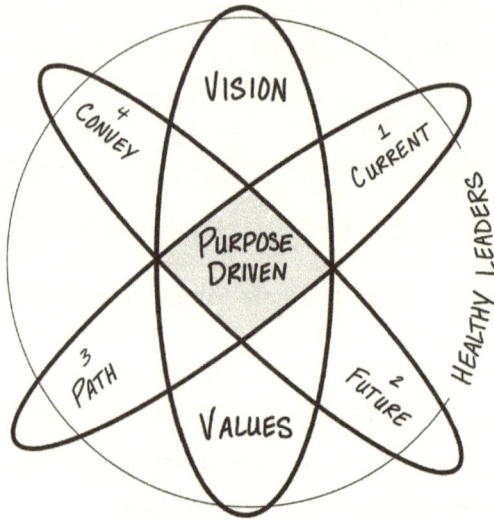

Part I: Current State

This part is all about diagnosing, gathering insights, and forming a clear picture of your business's current state. Each one of these items is an action step you should do to understand your business. You will be amazed at how collecting this information will change your perspective. Here's how you can break it down:

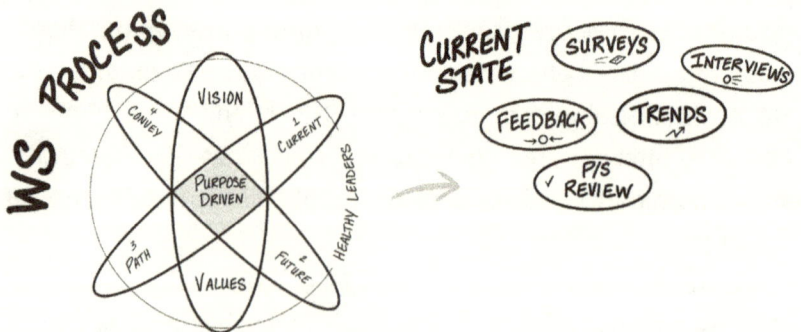

Survey: *Boots on the Ground*

Surveys are often dreaded, but when used intentionally, they can be incredibly valuable. Gather insights from 2 key sources: external (customers, vendors, suppliers, etc.) and internal teams (employees, partners, etc.). *Boots on the ground,* might not always have access to participation, so make it simple. Set up a tablet or laptop on location for them. Here are some questions to ask your employees:

1. What's the biggest headache you deal with in your role, and how can we help fix it?
2. Do you feel like your voice is heard? Be honest—how well do we act on feedback?
3. If you had a magic wand and could change one thing about working here, what would it be?
4. Looking back over the past year, what's one thing we've totally nailed?

After surveys, you'll want to do something more personable—interviews.

Interviews with Leaders

These aren't formal like hiring interviews but informal, productive conversations. They provide valuable facetime with your key leaders. They often reveal information you wouldn't get any other way. If time is tight, focus on areas of your business that are critical or facing immediate challenges. Here are some questions:

1. What's keeping you up at night about the business, and what's one thing we could do to make it better?
2. If we gave you a magic *fix-it* button for one challenge in your department, what would you use it on first?

3. If you had an unlimited budget for 1 initiative this year, what would you invest in, and how would it change our business?

Product and Service Review

Some of these *current state* items can be done at the same time—they're flexible but needed steps. Whether you offer a service or a tangible product, it's critical to consistently evaluate quality, competitiveness, and efficiency. Compare your offerings to competitors, track rework metrics (time and resources spent correcting mistakes), and identify ways to improve. Competition isn't your enemy; it's your ally in sharpening and refining what you do best.

Trends Review

Research industry trends on a regional, national, and global level. Network with peers and use research tools like Google Scholar. By making this a regular habit rather than a one-off task, you'll not only gather valuable insights but also develop your leader's analytical skills.

Feedback & Other Areas for Review

Other critical areas to analyze include marketing and sales performance, operational efficiency, employee development, turnover rates, and current strategic plans. While we won't dive into these in depth, they're worth reviewing as you plan for the future.

Don't fear the time investment. You're probably thinking, *This sounds like a lot of work.* Yes, it requires time, but not as much as you might think. This isn't a burden for 1 person to carry alone. Delegate responsibilities to your team. It's a powerful way to develop their skills. Better yet, think of this *not* as a 1-time annual process but as part of an ongoing rhythm. By breaking the work into manageable pieces, strategy becomes a natural part of your operations rather than a once-a-year scramble.

Part II: Desired Future

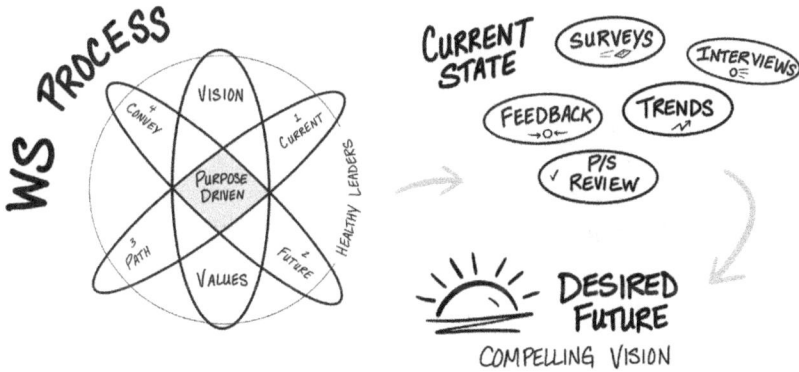

Revisit Your Vision

Your Vision, made up of your Always and Horizon Vision, serves as the guiding light for your strategy (hence why it's on top of the flower power sketch—it's like the north star of your strategy). Revisit this vision with leaders to ensure it remains clear, actionable, and compelling. Your leaders will be the ones cascading it throughout the company. Here are 3 important reflective questions to review with your leaders:

1. Is our current Always and Horizon Vision still clear, relevant, and inspiring?
2. Are we fully aligned with the vision, and are we effectively communicating and reinforcing it? Provide some evidence of how it's showing up in our work.
3. What key adjustments or strategic shifts are needed to ensure we stay on track toward achieving our vision?

Every year you will want to ensure that it is still true and relevant.

Part III: The Path Forward

In order to create a clear path, you should break it down into 3 sessions:

1. Review
2. Reflect
3. Render

Each of these sessions is meant to help form your Winning Strategy. These are called sessions because it's time for you to begin putting all the Current and Desired Future pieces together, then begin forming it into an executable plan. They should be formal and more structured.

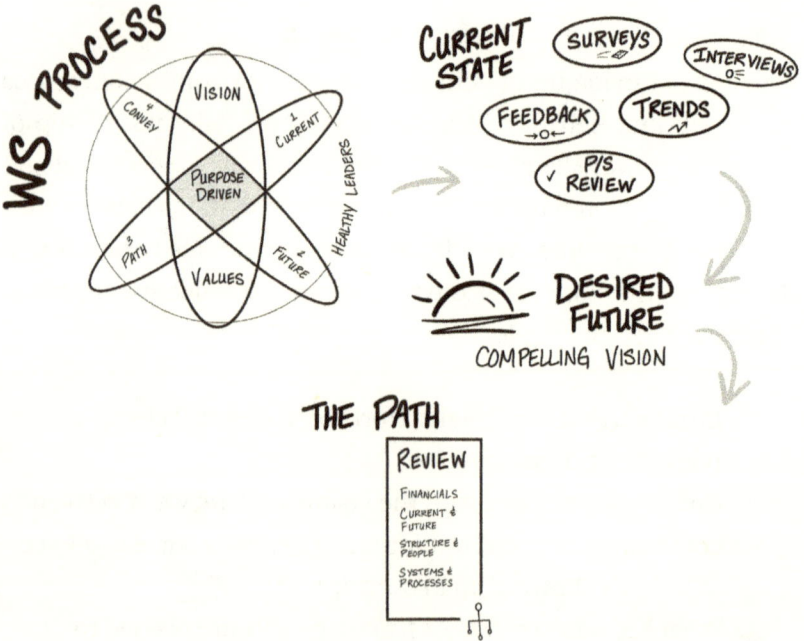

Session 1: Review

Have you ever filled out a survey or been a part of a group discussion, you gave thoughtful feedback, but then 6 months later, you had no idea what was done with it? This session is to close the loop and show your team that their input matters. You should analyze and discuss all the information that was collected during the Current and Desired Future sections. You will want to ensure everyone knows that it's *discussion mode*, not *decision mode* at this point. Encourage open dialogue and ask probing questions. Review the information, but don't make decisions based on it. That comes later.

FINANCIALS

First, you should review financials as a team. This is an obvious one, but in a nutshell, how profitable are you? There are many ways you can be more profitable, here are a few that should be reviewed as options:

- **Increase Pricing**: Evaluate opportunities to increase the cost of your products and services.
- **Sell More**: Identify ways to increase sales of your current offerings.
- **Operations Efficiency**: Increase efficiencies of products and services.
- **Faster AR**: Get paid faster for products and services through Accounts Receivables.
- **Slower AP**: Pay out slower through Accounts Payable.
- **Decrease Direct Costs**: Decrease money paid for supplies and labor of products and services.
- **Shrink Inventory**: Decrease the amount of inventory on hand.

CASH FLOW

One of the key components of financial review is cash flow management, which ensures your business has enough liquidity to cover expenses and invest in opportunities. By regularly reviewing a cash flow statement, which tracks cash inflows and outflows over time, businesses identify patterns, predict potential shortfalls, and make informed decisions to sustain operations. Turning this into a goal means setting specific benchmarks for cash reserves and creating strategies to maintain consistent cash flow, such as timely invoicing and better payment terms.

EXPENSES

Controlling expenses is critical for maintaining financial health. You can achieve this by evaluating current expenses, cutting unnecessary costs, and improving operational efficiency. Setting a goal here might involve identifying 3 key areas for cost reduction or establishing a percentage decrease in overall expenses.

Each of these components reviewed will help later during the Render Session, creating goals that will go on your Winning Strategy. The main areas to ensure you write down, when ready, are:

1. Revenue Goal
2. Cash Flow Goal (per month)
3. Net Profit Goal
4. Cash Reserves Goal

Whatever gets written down can be tracked.

CURRENT FEEDBACK

This is where you begin piecing everything together, including surveys, interviews, your vision, product and service review, and trends. You are looking for the obvious and not so obvious correlations. For example, maybe in your product review you noticed that there were some inconsistent quality problems. There could be many things to discuss like culture, quality control, and employee motivation per their job, to name a few. As a team, you will want to just review, not necessarily solve any problems just yet.

STRUCTURE & PEOPLE

With growth comes complexity, and complexity kills growth. The Structure and People Review is about reviewing your org chart together, ensuring that it still makes sense and operating well. It's also about evaluating your people to see if they are in the right seats per their skills, talents, and motivations. A lot of problems we face boil down to structure and people. Here are key questions to ask:

1. **"Do we have an org chart that clearly communicates who reports to who?"** It can be easy to forget to update and clarify as you grow.

2. **"Is everyone on the right seat of the bus?"** Author Jim Collins famously made this phrase meaningful. As you grow, you will want to review if people are using their God-given skills and talents effectively and in the right seat.

3. **"Do our leaders share and encompass our values?"** Believe it or not, people change. Of course they do, we all do, but when it comes to your business, we need to consistently realign our people with our values.

4. **"Do our leaders share and encompass our vision?"** This question isn't asking if they know it—it's asking if they actually share it and embody it. Do they want it?

SYSTEMS & PROCESSES

We'll discuss this in the Systems chapter in more detail, but at the end of the day, your systems and processes are only as good as the people running them. Whatever the input is will determine the quality of the output. *Systems* are the workflows for your business. *Processes* live within systems. *Technology* has become one of the biggest pieces of systems. You might be missing out if you are still trying to update that spreadsheet and share it every week. Here are some key questions to ask:

1. **"Where are the 'roadblocks' in our company?"** Review the areas where there are too many obstacles and constraints that slow down your work.

2. **"Where do we see inconsistency or redundancy?"** Review the parts of the company that don't have a consistent good outcome as you expected.

3. **"What can we make more efficient?"** We should be looking for ways to streamline operations. Oftentimes, this is tech related and requires some exploring to see what can be automated. Other times, it's simpler, like scripts for customer response emails or buying multiple hand tools, so that Jimmy doesn't have to drive and deliver someone a specific tool.

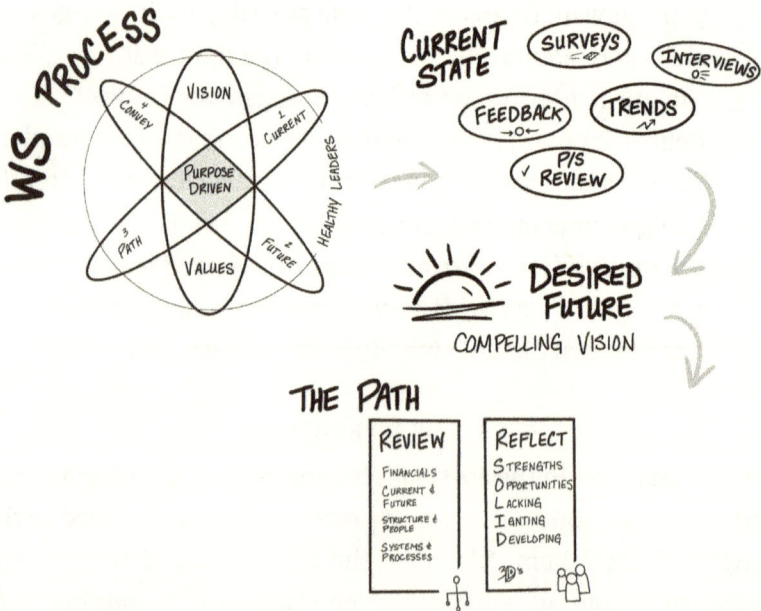

Session 2: Reflect

Now remember, these are sessions with your leaders. The point is to Review, Reflect, and Render information into a Winning Strategy. The

Reflect Session is where your team works on current state exercises together and reflects on strengths and development opportunities.

GET SOLID: CLARITY EXERCISE

This is the collaboration work. You want to take all the captured information and feedback from all areas of your business and collaborate on key SOLID questions. I created this exercise to help leaders reflect on key elements, but also not forget about objectives that were already in the works. Remember the overtaxing piece? This exercise is a powerful tool, and, if done right, you'll have taken all the inspirations, thoughts, and chaos and put them to paper. Here are the questions to ask:

1. **Strengths**: "What are the strengths of our business?" List out as many as you can think. You should not only know your strengths, but you should know how to continue to build on them. It's also important to ask why you think it's a strength. What evidence do you have?

2. **Opportunities**: "What are opportunities inside and outside of the business?" Opportunities are anything from marketing to employee development to trends you see in your industry. For example, if you are mostly selling directly to the customer, but you see an opportunity to sell directly to businesses, write it down!

3. **Lacking**: "What are we lacking in the business and need very soon?" This could be as simple as new fleet vehicles or more complicated like integrating a new software for your accounting. The key here is that you're listing out things in the near term that needs done. Basically, you are finding items that costs will need to be allocated to very soon.

4. **Igniting**: "What *fires* are just getting started?" You will want to list the objectives that you are already working on that take significant resources like people, time, and money. Knowing this will help you not overtax yourselves into doing too much. You want to be cognizant of where you already have "fires" starting.

5. **Develop On**: "What things should we continue to work on?" From your list of *Igniting*, you'll want to discuss as a team the objectives that still need to be pursued. At this stage, you want to transfer the relevant ones from the *Igniting* column and add them to *Develop On*. This is where you find out how many *fires* need to still stay a blaze, so you have a clear view of what to continue and how to allocate your resources.

STRENGTHS
Build On

OPPORTUNITIES
Inside & Outside Company

LACKING
Need Very Soon

IGNITING
Fires Getting Started

DEVELOP ON
Continue

This exercise should take some time to really think through and review all the collected information. Leaders should be willing to question what's unclear, say the hard truths, reflect on prior objectives and see where progress has been made, and so on. When your leaders have listed out as many things as applicable, it will be time to narrow the listed items.

Here is the method we teach to help narrow down on the listed items from the SOLID exercise:

DECISION, DISTRACTION, OR DEDICATION (3 D'S)

At this point, you could have a plethora of items listed like certain industry trends, big software upgrades, operational efficiencies, equipment purchases, territory expansions, etc. Choices need to be made! As a team, circle in blue which items you can make a decision on soon. These normally don't take time, mostly just a *decision* from the appropriate person. This could be as simple as the decision to hire a new employee, investing in additional software, etc. All blue circled items don't need a decision now but can be made in the near future. Write next to each blue circled item the name of who should make each decision. Essentially, these items don't need a strategy or objectives. They just need a decision. Then, you can move to distractions.

Blue = DECISION SOON

Red X = DISTRACTION

Green = DEDICATE

Put a red "X" on the items that are *distractions*—things you could work on, but will most likely just be a distraction at this point. The brilliant Michael Porter, Harvard business professor and author of many strategy books, says, "The essence of strategy is choosing what not to do." Your team will need to cross off what not to do. These items will often take time to "X," since your leaders may disagree on which items are important and which are not. In general, if you don't believe it will help you move toward your vision, then "X" it off the list.

Once you've gone through that, separately, indicate with a green circle which items you want to *dedicate* time and energy to the most. These will most likely be objectives you put on your final Winning Strategy. At the end of this session, you should know which objectives you really want to pursue as a company because your team believes it will *move the needle*. They will propel you closer to your vision.

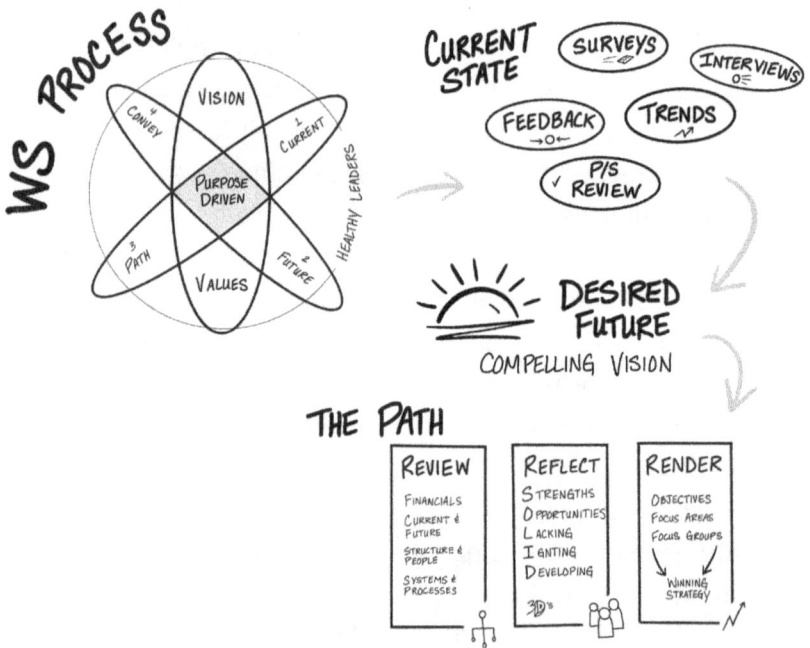

Session 3: Render

This session's goal is to put a draft together of your Winning Strategy. This is where you create objectives attached to your vision. Remember, these sessions can be done consecutively or spread out, but regardless of how you plan them, the goal of each session should be understood: Review, Reflect, and Render.

OBJECTIVES

At this point, you should have some objectives you believe will help you move toward your vision. For example, if you are working toward being a top 100 wholesale distributor, you will need to decide which objectives will truly help you get there. This could be investing in an e-commerce site, it could be key hires, and even operational efficiencies like process development. The objectives you create will come directly from all the work you've done to this point.

RENDER, FOCUS AREAS

Once you know some of the objectives, you will want to find some commonalities. The goal is to find the broad areas that help the company communicate what you're planning to work on. This part really helps with clarity if done right. There are many *mountains* that we can climb, but you should pick only the few that you believe will propel you toward your vision.

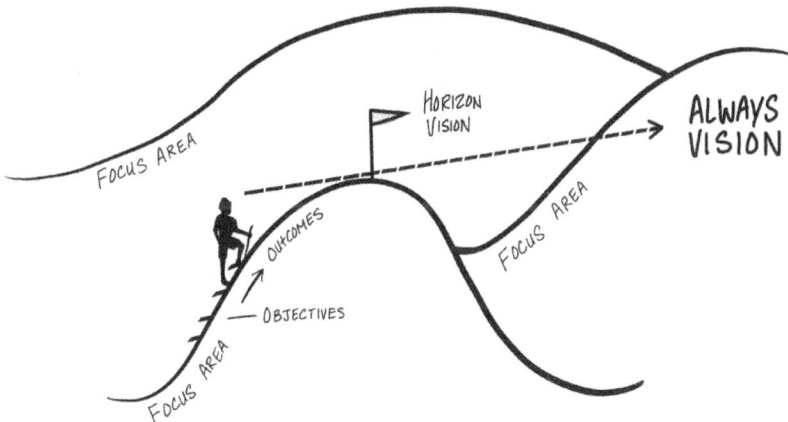

Here's an example:

I worked with a company that had many important objectives like employee training, improving onboarding, and developing high potential employees with 1:1 mentoring. It was apparent that 1 of their Focus Areas that year was *People Development*. Moving those objectives under that Focus Area allowed for better communication and for the leaders helping drive those objectives. Focus Areas should always lead to your vision and be attached to them. For this company, *People Development* was directly tied to their vision of expanding into new territories. Once you identify your Focus Areas, it also forces your team to pick and choose on the objectives.

Then, write the key outcomes per quarter for each objective. We'll talk more about this in the Outcomes chapter, but essentially, we want to know what will tell us that we are winning. I suggest you only have a few objectives under each Focus Area. Beyond that, you will be overloaded, which will lead to *overtaxing* your team. Your leaders should be updating their objectives monthly and reviewing them on a quarterly basis.

THE COMMON QUESTION

One question I hear often is: "Do you really expect our employees to do work outside their daily responsibilities?" In short, the answer is yes. Most of the objectives under your Focus Areas will be tied to helping them be more efficient, productive, and lead to more opportunities. You are teaching your employees how to manage strategic work that leads to your vision. This will help form a culture of results-driven teams that enjoy using their skills and talents while being held accountable.

WINNING STRATEGY

LOGO

Values shape
our beliefs,
thoughts,
and actions

VALUES CENTRIC

- Half truth is cowardly
- It is wiser to find out than suppose
- Humor is mankind's greatest blessing
- Continuous improvement over delayed perfection
- Don't depend on your eyes when your imagination is out of focus

CLARITY

What We Do

Who We Help

How We Do It

PURPOSE DRIVEN

HORIZON VISION

ALWAYS VISION (10+ yrs)

Characteristics/Desires/Big Goals

1.

2.

3.

4.

5.

Revenue Goal:

CORE PROMISES

ALWAYS **MEASURABLE & CONSISTENT**

1.

2.

Focus Area 1 (Title)	Focus Area 2 (Title)	Focus Area 3 (Title)
The Why:	The Why:	The Why:
1-1	**2-1**	**3-1**
Driver:	Driver:	Driver:
Team:	Team:	Team:
Objective:	Objective:	Objective:
Key Outcomes:	Key Outcomes:	Key Outcomes:
Q1	Q1	Q1
Q2	Q2	Q2
Q3	Q3	Q3
Q4	Q4	Q4
1-2	**2-2**	**3-2**
Driver:	Driver:	Driver:
Team:	Team:	Team:
Objective:	Objective:	Objective:
Key Outcomes:	Key Outcomes:	Key Outcomes:
Q1	Q1	Q1
Q2	Q2	Q2
Q3	Q3	Q3
Q4	Q4	Q4

Yearly Financial Goals (Tied to Vision & Focus Areas)

Revenue Goal:
Cash Flow Goal:
Net Profit Goal:
Cash Reserves Goal:

Leaders to Invest in the Next Year

1. (Name)–Development Opportunities:
2. (Name)–Development Opportunities:
3. (Name)–Development Opportunities:
4. (Name)–Development Opportunities:
5. (Name)–Development Opportunities:

Filter the "Objectives" into personal goals

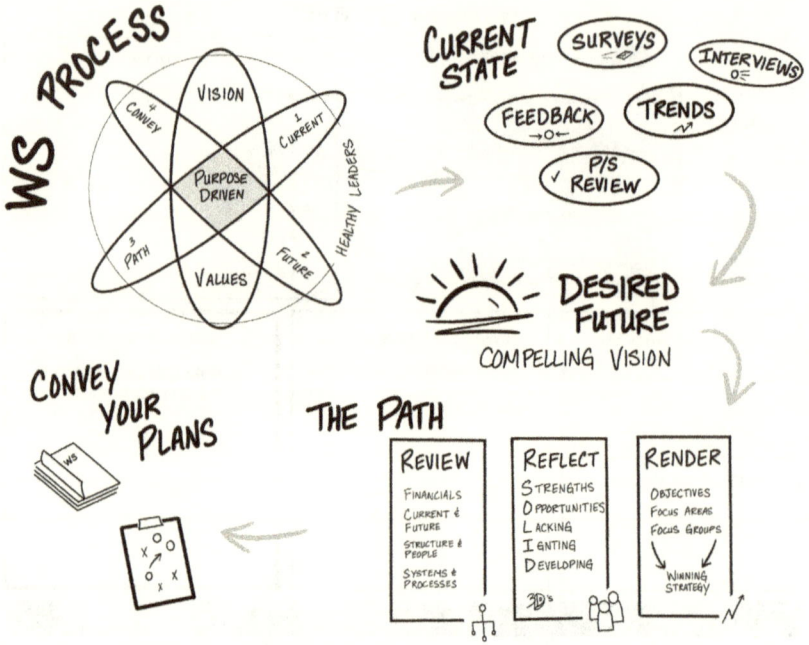

WS PROCESS

VISION
CONVEY
CURRENT
PURPOSE DRIVEN
HEALTHY LEADERS
PATH
FUTURE
VALUES

CURRENT STATE — SURVEYS — INTERVIEWS
FEEDBACK — TRENDS
P/S REVIEW

DESIRED FUTURE
COMPELLING VISION

CONVEY YOUR PLANS

THE PATH

REVIEW
FINANCIALS
CURRENT & FUTURE
STRUCTURE & PEOPLE
SYSTEMS & PROCESSES

REFLECT
Strengths
Opportunities
Lacking
Igniting
Developing

RENDER
OBJECTIVES
FOCUS AREAS
FOCUS GROUPS
WINNING STRATEGY

Part IV: Convey Your Plans

Now you have a draft of your Winning Strategy. Hopefully, at this point, you can see that it's becoming holistic. You should have your foundational items listed on the first page. That brings you to your second page, which reveals your Focus Areas.

All the Focus Areas and objectives that fall under those are what you believe you need to work on for the next year or so. Each of those objectives should be clearly linked to your vision. After it's all put together, you'll want to go through some key questions to ask as leaders:

- "Who's the 'driver' of the Winning Strategy?"
- "Have we taken on too much, is it reality to achieve this in our time frame?"
- "What resources will we need to achieve this?"

- "What obstacles will keep us from achieving this?"
- "What will be the distractions we need to pay attention to?"
- "How will we know if we are really on track?"

Communicate to Activate

Create a plan to communicate to employees the information that helps them know what you want to achieve and how you plan on doing it. This is where I see leaders slip. They've put together these grand plans and then, let it collect endless dust that is somewhat removed after *every* monthly cleaning. Communicating your strategy is a good form of accountability. Though, you will need other forms to stay disciplined. Here are some key questions to ask to ensure you've thought about your communication:

1. **"What information needs to stay in the room and why?"** Some information might be confusing to employees and distract them.
2. **"What objectives are tied directly to our employees' daily jobs?"** Be sensitive to anything that might make employees panic. An example of this might be automation or new software: "There goes my job!"
3. **"What is unclear? Is there any ambiguity at this point?"**
4. **"Do the Focus Areas show a direct link to our vision?"** Ensure that the plan is connected to what's on the horizon.
5. **"What do you expect from certain employees?"** State if it's high involvement, support expected, or leadership in certain areas.

Strategy is a process, and the process reveals your strategy. This process helps reveal and bring to surface things that you otherwise would not do without a system. I don't recommend you try doing this whole process in 1 shot. Make it a part of your leader's rhythm throughout the year. Your Winning Strategy will be integrated and flexible as part of your culture and operation.

GIVE PEOPLE A REASON TO TAKE THE WHEEL

We can't just make a list of to-dos and expect great things to happen. If we don't have goals that stretch us, then we will ultimately just hit the status quo. I know, I know, this is a hard balance, kind of like the overtaxing-versus-inertia scale. No matter which side of the scale you typically lean toward, *checking boxes* will ultimately lead to complacency. We need to help our people take ownership of the plans.

I've never experienced such *ownership* as I did at Weigand Construction Incorporated. Known as a premier general contractor, the company was where I learned from the best-hearted people. They weren't always known as the premier contractor. They had to build their way to the top and keep it like any other great company. When I started with the company, I was green as a dollar bill—I came on the scene right as their growth was ramping up. They housed multiple individuals with 20+ years at the business. They weathered the storms of 2008 and saw tremendous growth thereafter. It was their mindset that prepared them for large and organic expansions, but the way they cultivated an ownership mindset was no accident. It started with the leaders. They surrounded themselves with smart, growth-hungry individuals that learned together. They encompassed the CEO Mindset, which is an acronym I teach to many leaders:

Create Strategic Thinkers

The *C* is to create strategic thinkers. It's a skill that most leaders need to learn with intentionality, time, and experience. Strategy is the art of planning and executing with the *right* information and people toward your vision. If you're not helping your leaders lift their heads, think about future possibilities, and foresee obstacles, you are not building strategic thinkers. We need leaders who can think for themselves, analyze, and find a path forward. We need people who consistently find problems to solve and strategize, not just taking care of what *lands on their desk.*

Engage Your Team

The CEO Mindset is not a game of individual approaches. It takes a team that starts with trust but paves the way to true collaboration. Yes, we want strategic thinkers, but helping your leaders achieve a Winning Strategy takes commitment and engagement. If you want to engage the team, you need your team to share their true thoughts.

When I observe team members wanting to say something, but don't, we know the leader needs to engage the team even more. I observe this often.

Your team should adopt the belief that until the team members speak into the idea, it is not yet a commitment. Caution here: this does not mean that you should give false promises. Don't lead them to believe that because their idea is heard that it will be the end-all. Also, we are not looking for consensus. If that was the goal, many teams would be stuck in a stalemate. We want to engage the team by inviting them into the strategy, because it will, no doubt, take more than just you to achieve.

Own Your Commitments

It's not uncommon for teams to be unclear about who is doing what, how it should be done, and by what time. I see strategic projects and meetings starting without a clear goal established, and inevitably, a team with a lot of disappointment and frustration. Owning your commitments is a holistic process that creates room for team members to participate and have accountability. Owning your commitments as a team takes clarity, ensuring that team members are aligned, and commitments are clear. Your team will need to be reminded of the commitment repeatedly. You will get stuck in the (–) Dismal Daily and Me Focused. You will need to remind each other of why the Winning Strategy is so important.

Helping your team adopt the CEO Mindset is about ownership, knowing that it takes intentional development to move in the right direction and see results.

TAKE-IT-WITH-YOU NOTE

If you take anything from this chapter, please-please-please, let it be that the market can only carry you so far. The truly thriving companies are putting time and intentionality into their Winning Strategy. But your strategy will not succeed if you do not have sufficient systems to help you operate in the daily mess. This is where profit is lost or gained. Let's dive into systems.

BONUS: HOBBY LOBBY GROWS WITHOUT LOSING ITS SOUL

Great strategy means staying true to who you are while adapting to the changes needed to stay competitive. It's not just about internal improvements. It's also about knowing what makes you unique and using that to bring meaningful value to your customers.

Hobby Lobby is a company that holds tightly to its values while evolving its business strategy to remain a leader in the retail space. They've maintained a strong identity through community engagement, offering in-store classes and building online platforms to connect creative customers. At the same time, they've made smart moves, like turning sustainability into a strategic priority and investing in employee wages and benefits to attract top talent.

Hobby Lobby's growth in e-commerce and digital marketing shows they're not stuck in the past. Rather, they're moving with their customers while staying grounded in who they are.

Strategy isn't about chasing trends. It's about aligning your values with smart decisions that keep you ahead of the curve and top of mind with your customers.

WHY WINNING STRATEGY?

1. Winning Strategy is a balance between inertia and overtaxing.
2. Strategy is a process. The process then reveals your strategy.
3. The Winning Strategy is about results led by your leaders, not a *shiny* 1-page document.

CAUTION

1. Don't make the process a once-a-year thing. Integrate it throughout the year to help keep a pulse and keep the process manageable.
2. Winning Strategy is not a *one-size-fits-all* model. Tailor it to your company and ensure it fits your needs.
3. Take ownership of your Winning Strategy. Learn to stretch your leaders and help them have the CEO Mindset.

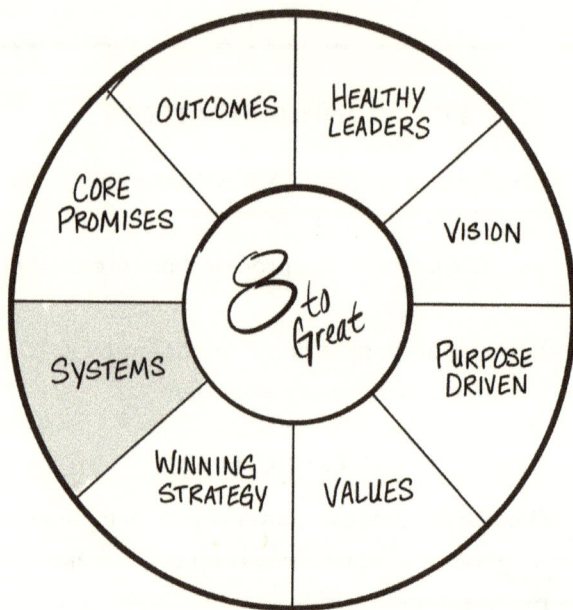

OUTCOMES

HEALTHY LEADERS

CORE PROMISES

VISION

8 to Great

SYSTEMS

PURPOSE DRIVEN

WINNING STRATEGY

VALUES

— SIX —
BUILD SUSTAINABLE SYSTEMS
How to Scale with Consistency

Continuous improvement is better
than delayed perfection.
—MARK TWAIN

OST BUSINESSES THINK they have the systems in place to scale effectively. But the reality is quite different. Over 50% of businesses we've worked with lack the clear, consistent way to grow with confidence. Take Terry for example. A former contractor who'd built and remodeled with nothing but a clipboard and a phone, Terry loved the idea of going digital. He had a Clint Eastwood feel, but surprisingly, had a knack for technology. He invested in every software he could find about 5 years into his business: project management tools, scheduling apps, estimating platforms, and a robust customer relationship system. His office became a display of dashboards and apps promising seamless operations. But behind the scenes, his team was struggling. With no clear processes and accountability in place, employees didn't know when or how to use the software. Some team members scribbled notes or defaulted to their own spreadsheets. A few of the boomers on staff, seasoned employees with decades of experience, flat-out refused to use the software. This meant they *silently* refused and did what they wanted instead. They couldn't see the value of logging every detail into a digital platform when a quick phone call or a handwritten note seemed faster. Without accountability or processes, the technology became siloed software, not fully connected systems. This disconnect between technology and true operational efficiency is all too common.

Building sustainable systems is crucial for scaling your business, but it requires more than just buying the latest tools. It demands a shift in mindset and a commitment to process. If you want your business to run with or without you, this chapter will show you how to build the structure to support it.

STOP REINVENTING THE WHEEL EVERY DAY

I've worked with many companies that had systems for portions of their business, like logistics or quality control, but lacked a way to tie them altogether for overall success.

Maybe you've said things like this:

- "Why after all these years, do we still do things differently?"
- "Why can't we get a rhythm? It seems like we're constantly running in circles."
- "If I want a job done right, it feels like I just need to do it myself."
- "They just do what they want, and I'm tired of it affecting other employees."

Many of us have said these very things, and most of them can be tied directly to how we operate our businesses. Within the Operational 4 of the 8 to Great—Winning Strategy, Systems, Core Promises, and Outcomes—are the components necessary for successful operations. Systems is the one that I see as an extreme—many companies rock at it, while others really struggle. I believe this to be for many reasons. One in particular is due to the personalities, talents, and skills of your leaders. There will be some who gravitate toward systems and processes, while some like other areas such as the people interaction side of your business. This is the art of balancing people and process. It's the skill of diversifying your team so that your systems are a natural fit. But regardless of who is on your team, and their personalities, I'll show you a way forward to have successful systems in your company.

This chapter will help you understand what systems are in more depth and how you can move toward creating and using them more successfully within your business. You will learn the starting point and key areas to begin revamping and building your own. I will also give you insightful ways to integrate processes into your systems. Whether you struggle or rock at them, read on, because this will help you level up no matter where you are.

Know the Difference. Run More Efficiently

Many people get systems and processes confused. A *system* is a group of technology, processes, functions, and people that work together to achieve a goal. They help make things more efficient, organized, and easier for decisions.

Mostly reliant on automation, input, discipline, and consistency, systems are typically technology driven and require processes for traction. John Maxwell once said, "Small disciplines repeated with consistency every day lead to great achievements gained slowly over time." Systems cannot lead to great achievements on their own. Processes are the consistent disciplines that help give systems their speed. A *process* is a series of specific steps or activities to complete a particular task, such as filling out an operational checklist or approving purchase orders. Processes are typically narrower in focus, providing consistency and efficiency.

SYSTEM

Processes are crucial for systems, much like how individual car components (processes) work together to create a fully functioning vehicle (system).

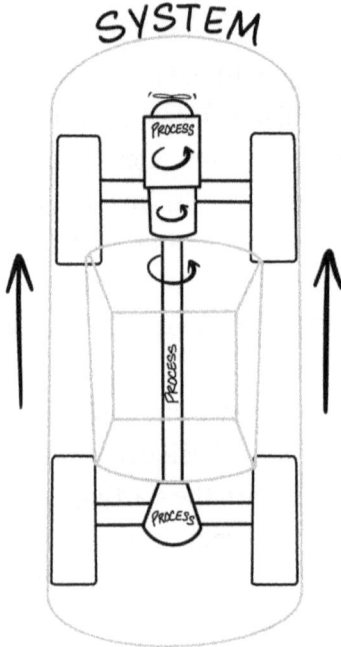

Clarity Is Kindness

Let's start with one of the starting points for system success—structure. Organizational structure is the functionality of your hierarchy and clarity for your people. It's the chain of command. One of the main parts of structure is organizational charts. This is for clarity of personnel reporting and key responsibilities. Though this seems basic, it's not uncommon to see highly profitable companies struggle in this area. There are many reasons why this might be. Here are a few combinations of why you could be held back by your org structure:

1. **Growth and People**: As your company has grown, employees have been asked to take on additional tasks beyond their normal responsibilities. Often, this also means *multiple* leaders are helping oversee multiple employees or functions of the company. We call this the Dotted Line Dilemma. This is where you have many

split roles or functions that end up showing 1 employee reporting to several leaders on an org chart. Often, depicted by the dreadful dotted line. The dilemma occurs when accountability is needed. It will be hard to know which leader should step in and how much control they have. Growth and people can be hard to navigate. It's not uncommon to see businesses with a scattered approach to who leads what and who.

2. **Growth and Speed**: The speed at which your company has grown leaves little room for planning and reorganizing structure. You've been strapped in and along for the ride. Years later, you realize your structure is not as clear as it should be, but it's hard to go back and clarify it. People may get used to the chaos and adopt it as a part of your culture.

3. **Lack of Knowledge**: You don't know what you don't know. One way this happens is when many tenure leaders grow up in the company. As a result, they lack experience in how to

navigate the needed structure. In essence, they only learn the business knowledge that exists within your current business. This means outside perspective is often lacking. Find non-competitive peers in your industry to understand how they've grown and developed different than you.

4. **Lack of Intention**: Maybe you have not created a rhythm to have intentionality for your chain of command. You might think it will work itself out, or possibly you don't think it's that big of a deal. I mean hey, revenue is still on the rise—why mess with the way you operate? Many small problems that are ignored will become big problems down the road, and often at the worst time.

Enhance Alignment

Maybe you related to more than 1 of those reasons. I suggest you review organizational structure at least annually to enhance clarity and alignment. When reviewing it, every function, title, and department can typically fit into one of these categories:

- Marketing
- Sales
- Operations
- Finance
- Human Resources
- Technology

I created this sketch to help businesses see the overall functions within an org chart and how they each support and integrate into each other. In our fast-paced business world, Human Resources (HR) and Technology are the support of all parts of your business.

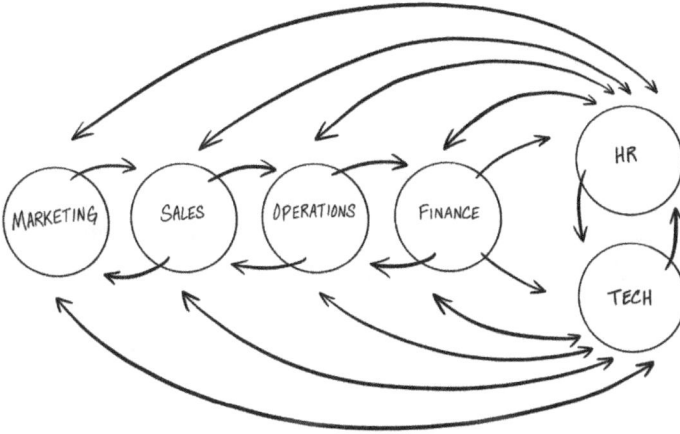

This doesn't necessarily mean you have a leader for each of those areas. Other alternatives are to organically grow leaders wearing multiple *hats* or outsource some roles with oversight. Before moving forward, I would like to say I hate using the term "Human Resources," but it is commonly recognized, so don't stop reading if you have the same disdain for it. In essence, it's how you find, develop, and align people within your business.

Human Resources—People

HR should be sectioned into 2 basic understandings: Operational and Developmental:

Operational HR

This category covers the day-to-day functions, focusing on maintaining smooth business operations and ensuring compliance. It includes recruiting, staffing, compensation, compliance, compliance training, legal, workforce planning, and health and safety.

Developmental HR

This category involves long-term planning and the development of your people. It focuses on aligning best practices with business goals and enhancing employee growth and engagement. It includes training, development opportunities, culture, managing performance, and strategic planning.

Technology—Enhance

Technology is a must in today's business world. None of the tech in our businesses is worth much unless we have the right people to manage it. Technology, along with Human Resources, is the support that keeps all of the areas of your business going. Technology can be sectioned into 2 basic understandings: Operational and Customer-Focused Technology.

Operational Technology

This category includes all technologies that help run the day-to-day functions of a business, streamline processes, and manage resources. It focuses on efficiency, productivity, and process management. Examples include computers, servers, software/applications, cybersecurity, workflow automations, etc.

Customer-Focused Technology

This category covers technologies that support long-term business strategies, enhance customer interactions, and provide insights for decision-making. Examples include training, email, video conferencing, e-commerce, chatbots, support systems, etc.

A strong company structure is the foundation of system success. Organizational structure provides chain of command clarity and functionality, helping teams understand reporting lines and key responsibilities. Though it may seem basic, even highly profitable companies can struggle with structure. To avoid pitfalls like the Dotted Line Dilemma, review your organizational structure annually to maintain alignment and clarity. By keeping structure intentional and regularly updated, you can ensure that every role and system contributes effectively to your overall success. You might be asking, "Beyond structure, what are the main systems I need in my business?"

THE SYSTEMS WHEEL

The Systems Wheel illustrates the essential systems every business will need as a foundation. Healthy Leaders are the central hub, uniting and empowering every key area of your business. Without them, your systems risk spinning into disarray, with disconnected processes and misaligned priorities. Your leaders will be the hub of all your required systems. There are 5 key systems that pivot on Healthy Leaders and are needed as the bare minimum for every business: Magnetic Marketing, Strategic Sales, Future-Focused Finance, Aligned Operations, and Outcomes.

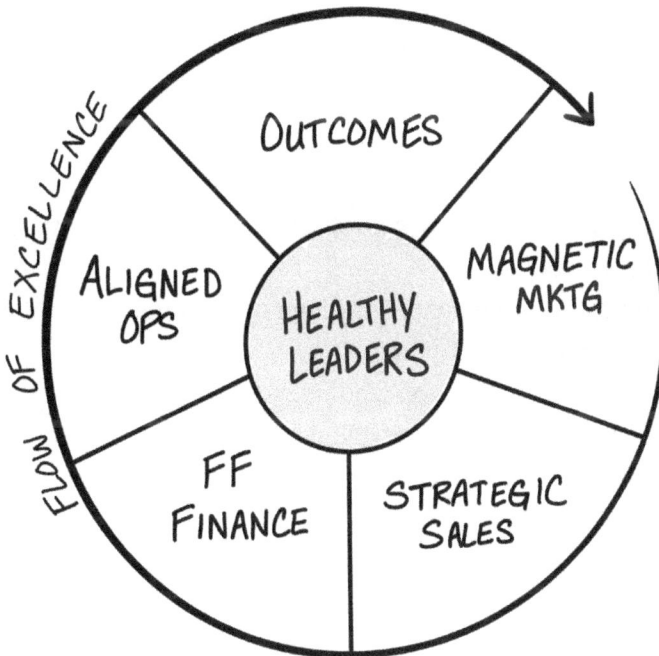

The following 5 sections provide a breakdown of each of the essential systems:

Magnetic Marketing

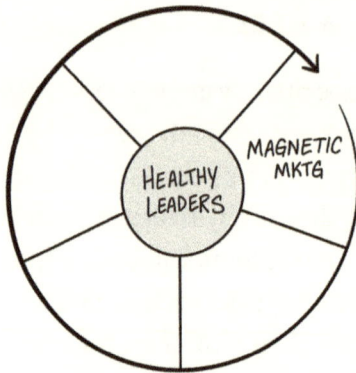

Magnetic Marketing is about attracting and engaging the right customers by communicating the company's purpose and values. Best-selling author, Seth Godin, says, "Everyone is not your customer." Magnetic Marketing is about finding *your* customers. It emphasizes authenticity and differentiation, ensuring that your business stands out in a crowded market. Even if your business is more dependent on relationships, marketing will help build trust by showing who you are and what you're about. Marketing is also the way your people carry themselves. They are the best marketers you'll ever hire.

Key Focus

- Build a strong brand that reflects the company's purpose and values.
- Connect with customers through storytelling and transparency.
- Have extreme focus on who you serve, why, and how you help them solve their problems.

Magnetic Marketing pulls customers toward your business and builds long-lasting relationships. Systems examples include Content management systems like Salesforce or HubSpot, marketing automation systems like Mail Chimp, and social media tools to help with connecting and messaging like LinkedIn Sales Navigator. There will be 100 new ones by the time you read this.

Of course, there are other marketing strategies and systems like customer events, ads, flyers, and sponsorships. Magnetic Marketing is about a system that combines all the right tools, processes, and functions to attract your customers. In many businesses and markets, this doesn't necessarily mean spending money on ads or flyers. It could be as simple as creating the right relationships and pursuing the right partnerships.

An Example of a Magnetic Marketing System

Your marketing automation software sends out emails to potential customers in your area. You have a link on that email to your social media and website. Hopefully, you have conversations with people and don't do that 3-email automated follow-up thing. You are in key relationship building peer groups like your local commerce group. Maybe you have a few billboards or digital ads or are in money-saving coupon books depending on your niche and market. You have a person who is in charge of filtering all leads to a call, quote, and whatever else helps break the ice and get you in front of the customer. The Connection Point is symbolic to show that all your systems should tie into each other for seamless integration, as shown in this sketch.

MAGNETIC MKTG

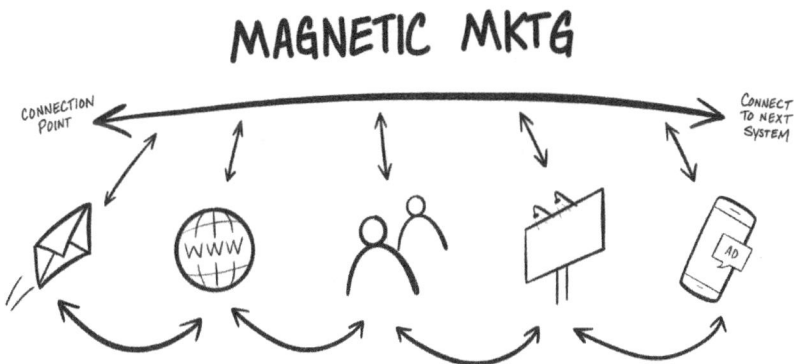

Strategic Sales

Strategic Sales focuses on delivering value to customers while driving revenue growth. It bridges the gap between marketing and operations, ensuring that the promises made in marketing are fulfilled during the sales process.

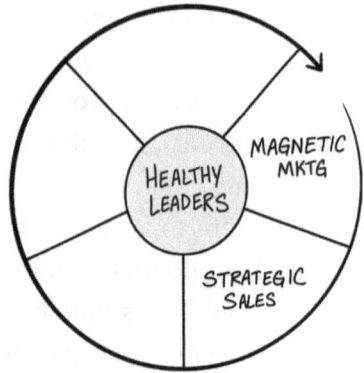

Key Focus

- Build relationships, not just closing deals.
- Train your people to understand and communicate value effectively.
- Track performance and adapting strategies based on feedback.

Strategic Sales turns prospects into loyal customers by delivering on your promises. Examples of things that are a part of this system include customer relationship management (CRM) software, e-commerce systems, generating leads, quoting or bidding systems, point-of-sale systems, forecasting tools, and, good ol' handshakes and conversations. Strategic Sales is not about getting everyone to do business with you; it's about strategically selling to the right customers. If you try to please everyone, you will inevitably be drowning yourself.

An Example of a Strategic Sales System

You have a CRM or spreadsheet to help track potential customers you are talking to and need to follow-up with. You have a script for all employees involved in customer relationships to help keep conversations focused. All of your sales personnel are equipped with resources like slide presentations, pamphlets, flyers, etc. You have a person who is in charge of filtering all leads to a call, quote, and whatever else helps break the ice to get you in front of the customer. You have a scripted email that goes to your customers after successful work and collect a testimonial to use on your website, social media, etc.

Future-Focused Finance

Future-focused finance ensures that your company's financial health supports its goals. This includes ensuring current finances are in order, while budgeting, forecasting, and resource allocation are aligned with long-term objectives. Having systems that help keep finances in check enables you to be future-focused and allocate resources toward your Winning Strategy.

Key Focus

- Create budgets that align with priorities that align with your vision and strategy.
- Manage cash flow to ensure operational continuity.
- Fund through smart financial planning and budgeting.

Finance is not just about numbers. It's about making decisions today that support your vision for tomorrow. There is plenty of software out there to help you manage your specific finance system like QuickBooks or industry-specific software. Ensuring your payroll is streamlined and you are getting paid in a timely manner are obvious first steps. To ensure it's holistic, you need to have processes and functions that work together.

An Example of a Future-Focused Finance System

The starting point will be your Winning Strategy, where you clearly have identified your vision and Focus Areas. This will reveal where you need to invest resources like people, time, and money. You have clear goals of what revenue you need for the year and what monthly cash flow you need, and it's written down. You have amazing, disciplined input into your finance tracking software, providing you key information.

You also have a monthly meeting with key leaders to discuss progress and find gaps like rework percentages and dips in monthly revenue. The future of finances is talked about often, taking all the information like potential projects and orders, and making a projection of what months in advance will look like. This enables you to budget and save resources needed for your Winning Strategy, things like expanding into a new territory or hiring a new key role. On a more granular level, you have a dedicated person or an automated program in charge of keeping on top of customers who still owe you money. You then balance that with payments that you owe to your suppliers, vendors, and partners. This could be tracked on your finance software or spreadsheet, depending on what is needed.

Aligned Operations

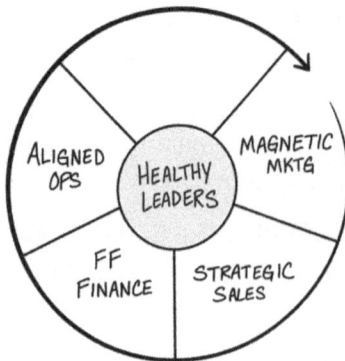

This is how the work gets done and determines if the business is running smoothly. Aligned Operations are essential for ensuring consistency, efficiency, and scalability. Beyond getting the work done with high quality, Aligned Operations is about ensuring you are executing the work in a timely and efficient manner, creating loyal customers.

Key Focus

- Streamline workflows to reduce inefficiencies.
- Leverage technology to optimize processes.
- Prioritize employee training and development to enhance execution.

Aligned Operations ensures that the business runs efficiently and without unnecessary friction. Examples of this system include project management systems, inventory management, quality control, training software, quoting and estimating software, and many more. This one is a bit more complex, as operations are different for each business on how things get done. For starters, it's helpful to start with an overall company workflow visual showing the process of how you operate within your business from beginning to end of your product and service.

This puts all the pieces of the puzzle together in one document.

An Example of an Aligned Operations System

Quoting goes to sales. That goes to project management, which coincides with production or installers. That then goes to customer approval and satisfaction. Then, a follow-up email for a testimonial. Obviously, if you are in manufacturing or other specific industries, your workflow will look different. Each of these makes up an operations system that can be technology driven like a project management software that helps track where you are at every step of the operational process. Or, it can be a series of processes that is used manually like checklists, written processes, and videos that help your employees know what to do every phase of the way.

The Aligned Operations system is about taking all the technology, processes, and functions required to help with clarity and run smoother. This reduces headaches for your employees and customers. Here's an example of a workflow from a friend and client of ours, simple and effective:

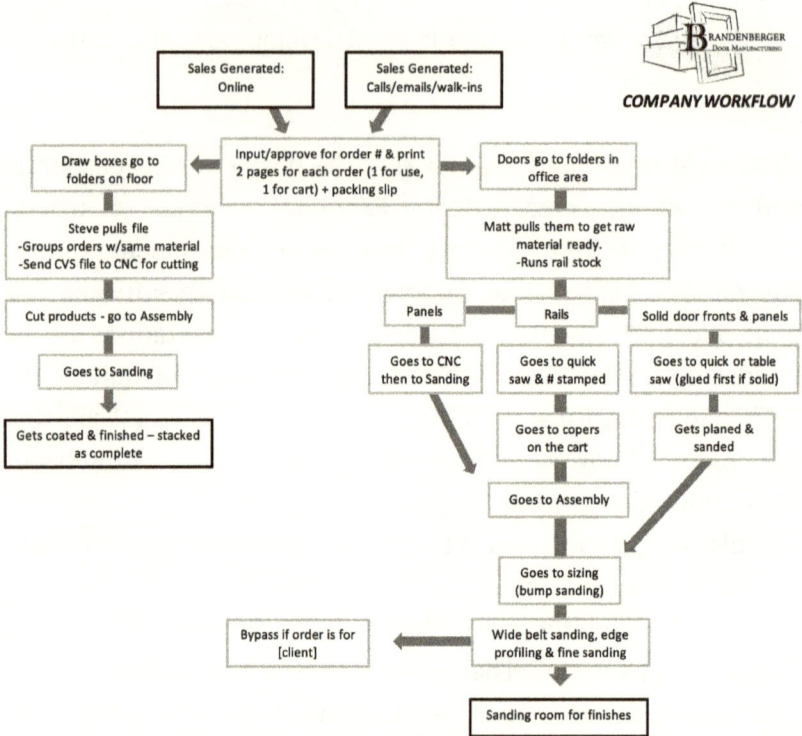

COMPANY WORKFLOW

Sales Generated: Online

Sales Generated: Calls/emails/walk-ins

Input/approve for order # & print 2 pages for each order (1 for use, 1 for cart) + packing slip

Draw boxes go to folders on floor

Doors go to folders in office area

Steve pulls file
-Groups orders w/same material
-Send CVS file to CNC for cutting

Matt pulls them to get raw material ready.
-Runs rail stock

Cut products - go to Assembly

Panels

Rails

Solid door fronts & panels

Goes to Sanding

Goes to CNC then to Sanding

Goes to quick saw & # stamped

Goes to quick or table saw (glued first if solid)

Gets coated & finished – stacked as complete

Goes to copers on the cart

Gets planed & sanded

Goes to Assembly

Goes to sizing (bump sanding)

Bypass if order is for [client]

Wide belt sanding, edge profiling & fine sanding

Sanding room for finishes

Aligned Operations creates a cohesive environment where every department and team member understands their role and how their work connects to the bigger picture. When operations are truly aligned, sales knows exactly what information to pass to project management, project managers seamlessly coordinate with production, and customer service has all the tools needed to ensure satisfaction. This alignment isn't just about efficiency. It's also about building a well-oiled machine that minimizes miscommunication, reduces errors, and increases profitability. For any business, Aligned Operations can be the difference between constant firefighting and proactive, strategic growth. It means that every step of the process, whether automated by software or managed manually, is designed to support the business's goals and deliver consistent, high-quality results.

Outcomes

In the Outcomes chapter, we'll share this in more detail, but in general here are the key components: Healthy Leaders, Winning Strategy, Team Outcomes, Employee Outcomes, Customer Outcomes, and Org Outcomes. Outcomes is a system where you have a way to track key results for your business and connect them together. Tracking results is about behavior, just as much as it's about numbers or data. For this system, you could use a spreadsheet or management software. Either way, the system is how you connect the key results of your company. Many software platforms will have their own results dashboard. The trick is to extract that data into your own system to review it comprehensively.

Key Focus

- Ensure that everyone from leadership to individuals, and from company to customer results is tracked.
- Each key area should have measurable results that are tracked with clear goals.
- All areas of your business are accountable to expectations and results creating a performance-driven culture.

Embracing Outcomes is not just about setting targets. It's also about creating a culture where measurable impact is at the heart of every decision. When businesses focus on outcomes, they transform from being busy to being effective. Most of us believe that busyness is a real threat, but yet, we will consistently do busy things that don't contribute to real results. Here are some short independent examples of Outcomes:

- **Healthy Leadership**: A construction company implements quarterly leadership development check-ins with executive team members, measuring growth in decision-making, delegation, and team meetings. Over 12 months, the check-ins reveal that managers are more focused on the development of their team. This is tracked in a human resource management system.

- **Winning Strategy**: A local landscaping business has a Focus Area to specialize in outdoor living spaces instead of general lawn care. With a clearer vision, they train their team around this specialty and start attracting bigger, more profitable projects. In 1 season, they go from doing 20 small jobs a month to 10 larger projects with more revenue. They meet monthly and track outcomes on their Winning Strategy document.

- **Team Outcomes**: A bakery expands into catering but finds orders getting mixed up. They start holding 10-minute team huddles each morning to review the day's events. This simple rhythm builds team coordination, and within a month, customer complaints drop by 30%, and staff say they feel more on the same page.

- **Employee Outcomes**: A home services remodel company encourages technicians to choose a personal goal each quarter—whether it's learning a new skill, improving communication, or mentoring a newer employee. These goals are tracked on a spreadsheet and updated monthly and placed in a shared drive for the employee.

- **Customer Outcomes**: A small-town gym notices some members stop showing up after a few weeks. Instead of ignoring it, they start personally calling those members to check in and offer encouragement or help. Attendance increases, and more members begin to share their positive experiences with a testimonial that is used on their website. They track these calls in a customer relationship management software.

- **Organizational Outcomes**: A custom furniture business wants to reduce waste. They start tracking how much material is left unused after each job and challenge the team to come up with creative ways to reuse it. Within a few months, waste is down by 50%, and the team starts making bonus products like cutting boards and side tables, some of which are sold or donated locally, improving both profit and community presence. This is tracked on their Winning Strategy document.

Flow of Excellence: The Role of Processes

Surrounding these 5 systems is the Flow of Excellence, which emphasizes the importance of processes in ensuring seamless collaboration and execution. This is the speedometer of your systems. Every system is

interconnected through these processes, which act as the momentum. The Flow of Excellence ensures that your business operates as a unified whole, not as isolated silos. They help bring clarity to your systems by ensuring that they are all connected and help give speed by giving instruction and consistency.

MAKE PROCESSES PEOPLE ACTUALLY WANT TO USE

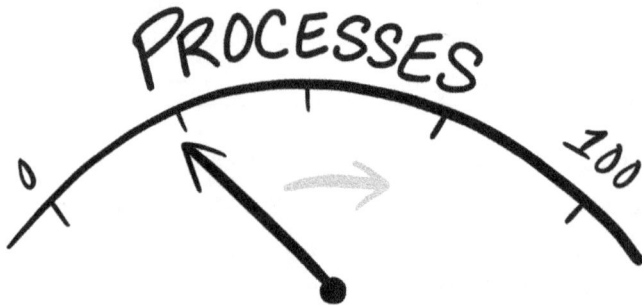

Since we've talked so much about systems, but also mentioned processes, let's focus on particularly what we mean by processes. When I work with companies, I hear one word that I loathe, SOPs. In case you need more here, it stands for standard operating procedures. Alright, it's not that they're bad. As matter of fact, systems need them to be successful, but they are often stale and get ignored. Hear me out, I am proposing that you think about processes a little differently. We do want a standard, but not to the effect where you only accept 1 type of process, like a written, flow chart, size 12 Times New Roman font, and paragraphs of words that no one will read. We want processes to be enjoyable, to have some freedom, and most of all, to be something that people actually use. Your systems depend on it! Here are the 4 types of broad processes that we think are the most important:

1. **Overall Workflow**: This is the workflow of an entire function or department. It is typically best depicted as some sort of flowchart and shows visually how 1 step is connected to the next. It starts at the beginning of how work comes into the department or function and carries onto the next. As stated earlier, I also recommend your entire company have a flowchart to visually depict the overall system. Picking one type of visual form will be important for teams to adopt a consistent look. This could be as simple as a spreadsheet with a legend for color, font, etc., or you could use 1 of the many software options.

2. **Specific Activity Workflow**: This is the same as above, with the exception it is more granular to a specific activity. Again, this is typically a visual representation, not just words on paper. An example of this might be how customer reps should direct customers to receive help for their questions. Another example would be how an engineer should pass on their drawings to a project manager and so forth. Each of these is a workflow that should be visually clear. Workflows can be combined with written form.

3. **Process Written Form**: This is where words on a paper are reserved for things that truly help with clarity. This could be checklists, instructional documents, summaries, lists, etc. SO... Ps fall into this category (hard to say that while typing this). Just be careful that they stay as *minimal* as possible. The more words you add, the more you must update when needed. And if you haven't noticed, there are less people that read and more that watch videos...

4. **Process Media Form**: This one is our favorite and has been our main method for helping others build processes. Media form is recording processes mostly by video, although we have seen audio as well (or heard, ha!). It's as simple as recording yourself and packaging it as an MP4 or link to a shared location. With many virtual call capabilities, like sharing screens, you can record a step-by-step guide on how to perform a task. You can even do this on just about any virtual call platform, just schedule one by yourself and hit record. It's also as easy as recording your team performing a task with your smartphone. It doesn't have to be complicated, and if your processes are only internal, you don't need the highest quality or resolution. It just needs to get the job done.

Regardless of the systems within your business, don't forget that they require clear processes. It's also important to understand that there are many types of processes, and all of them should connect alongside each other and feed into your systems.

3 PHASES TO SYSTEM CREATION

Creating good systems can be understood in 3 major phases: diagnose, form, and integrate...repeat. I'll stop here and ensure we're on the same page. A *system* is a group of technology, processes, functions, and people that work together to achieve a goal. They help make things more efficient, organized, and easier for decisions.

Creating good systems in your business requires that you understand which ones you need, form a bridge to help with connectivity, and integrate them into the overall company. The Systems Wheel gives clarity to essential systems for most businesses, but there are more systems required for many businesses. Building the right ones for your company is not something that happens overnight, but will come together with consistency.

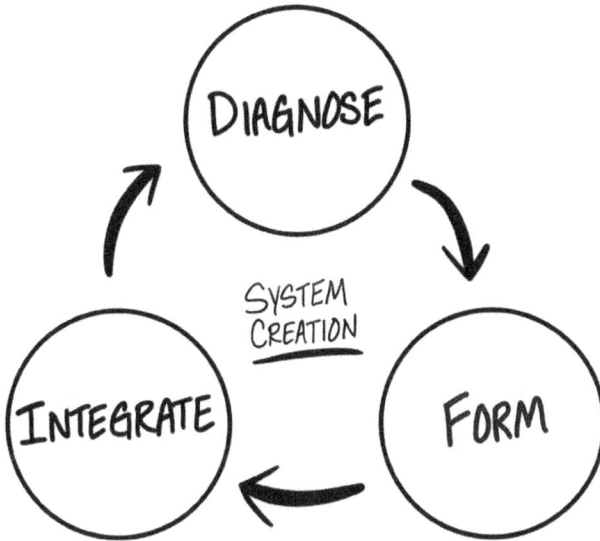

1. Diagnose Current Opportunities

This is where you explore your current operations to see where you have inconsistencies and failures. Using peers and successful businesses as an example can be a great way to discover areas of growth for your systems. Diagnosis is mainly about exploring where you see disconnects in your company, maybe that's by product failure, operational inconsistencies, customer complaints, or the percentage of rework required in a given period of time. It's also to investigate what is working really well, explore what you can replicate or build on. Diagnosis is best achieved with many people, not a few. Getting key leaders involved to give input will help reveal those broken links faster. Diagnosis is the starting point. Don't try implementing or fixing something too quickly, or move after hearing 1 frustrating comment. Dig deeper to understand.

2. Begin Forming Systems

Forming is the way you take technology, processes, information, supporting documents, etc. and make it a system. This may take time, but it's always worth it. Here's an example: within HR, you might have many functions that fall within a system like safety training, personnel development, personal goals, reviews, etc. Each of those functions might have their own processes, like how to record training, scheduled classes for development, written goals with progress updates, and reviews that are tracked. Each of those is a process that helps build a system, but they truly aren't a system until there is connectivity to bring them together. Processes on their own often look and feel disconnected or clashing.

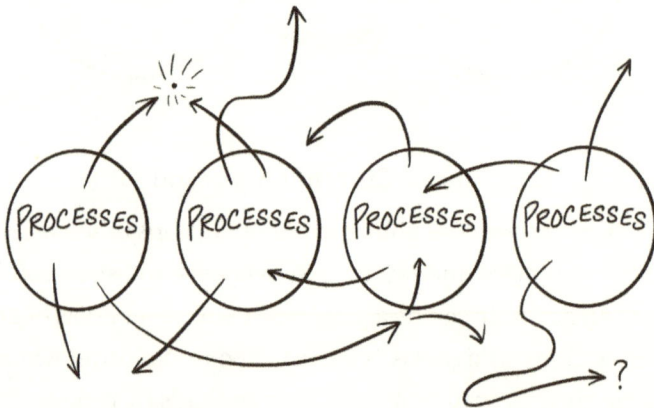

Processes need to connect in order to have a high level of productivity and efficiency. Maybe that's a spreadsheet with employee's information in one spot, or possibly it's a software that connects multiple systems into one. Forming is a very important part of creation, and it should be tested and reviewed before truly implemented.

Another important aspect of Forming is to extract. You need to record and extract the knowledge of your experienced employees.

This is often skipped in the forming phase because it takes time. Don't go another minute without extracting the *tribal knowledge* that exists within your business. Doing that is often viewed as messy. I've heard people say they don't want to make others feel pushed out or unneeded. This is where leaders can effectively communicate why it's important to record people's knowledge and have discussions about sustainability. Turn their wisdom into a repeatable, scalable system that strengthens your business for the long haul.

3. Integrate Systems Well

Integration is taking all the processes, tools, people, and technology and integrating them into your operations. This is often the phase that gets messed up for many reasons, but one in particular is because we sometimes focus on the process more than the people. We don't think about the buy-in needed. Sometimes we become too concentrated on the parts and processes we might think we have this grand system that will maximize results, but then forget that Ted over in accounting hates change. *Schucks!* How could we forget about Ted? In my experience, bad systems integrations is one of the biggest indirect costs in companies. Whether that's a new software or a new way to fill out a spreadsheet and submit it, either way, Ted wants to give his thoughts—*buy-in*.

Systems integration starts with leaders who ensure they're creating good opportunities for others to chime in. When systems are integrated well, multiple processes will flow from 1 activity to the next and feed into a larger system, one that connects workflow from beginning to end. For great systems, ensure your people know how and why the system will help them in their jobs. If you don't, you might risk team members not truly buying in, which leads to wasted money and time, or worse, their frustration and departure.

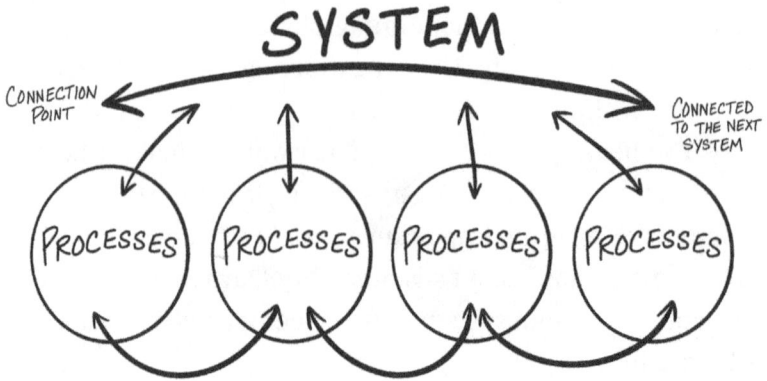

EMPOWERMENT STARTS WITH A GOOD SYSTEM

You might be asking, what's on the other side of systems? What do they do besides create sustainability? Directly tied to systems is the ability to empower. The ability and willingness to empower others can, and hopefully is, one of the direct outcomes of good systems. When your systems and processes are alive and connected, it breeds opportunities for leaders to empower.

Think about it, at one point, you probably had very little systems and processes in your business, which made it hard to give responsibilities to others. They had nothing to go off of. Normally, the starting point was, "Hey, why don't you just be attached to my hip for a while and learn the ropes?" Remember when you had to do that?

Often, we will ask the question to leaders during workshops, "Who here considers themselves an expert in what they do?" Many will raise their hands, which is great because you want people to own their expertise. Then we'll ask, "How many of you would say you're an expert in empowering your employees to also become experts?" Not surprising, but very few will raise their hands. We can't just be experts in our field. We should want that for our teams too. What keeps us from empowering our employees? There are many reasons, but maybe it's because:

- We lack trust in others.
- We desire control or just can't let go.
- We struggle with being a perfectionist.
- It could be time constraints.
- We could lack knowledge in how to do it. Or maybe we don't have the right systems to empower correctly?

Or possibly, it's the worst one of them all—the company has built a culture of it being more noble to do everything yourself. That means if your most influential people in your business are not empowering, then it will likely not be the norm for others. Systems should and will, if done correctly, empower your future leaders. If we're not actively empowering our teams to become experts, we're not just missing an opportunity; we're holding our businesses back. When leadership clings to control or perfectionism, it creates a bottleneck that stifles growth and innovation.

But imagine a culture where people feel trusted, equipped, and encouraged to step up. Where systems are in place to guide, support, and elevate each other. This is how great businesses transform into a self-sustaining company—by building a legacy of capable, confident experts at every level.

TAKE-IT-WITH-YOU NOTE

Systems are built on a mindset of continual improvement, not perfection. It starts with the overall structure and is integrated with processes as the conduit that keeps momentum. They help improve productivity, streamline operations, and support decision-making. Technology has become a big part of good systems.

BONUS: HOW TRADER JOE'S TURNED LESS INTO MORE

Trader Joe's proves that simplicity isn't just a virtue. It's also a powerful component of business systems. Unlike traditional grocery stores that carry tens of thousands of items, Trader Joe's limits its product selection to about 4,000 carefully chosen goods, most under its private label. This intentional limitation streamlines every aspect of their operations, from supply chain to shelf stocking. It reduces decision fatigue for customers, strengthens vendor relationships, and simplifies inventory management. The result? Lower costs, higher quality control, and an experience that feels curated and consistent across every store.

What makes Trader Joe's systems remarkable is that they're built for people, not just processes. Regular shipments keep stores stocked and fresh, while repeatable workflows empower employees to focus on customer service rather than backend chaos. There's no unnecessary complexity—just clear routines that run like clockwork.

This kind of system simplicity fuels sustainability. It's a reminder that effective systems aren't about doing more; they're about doing what matters, better. Like Trader Joe's, your company can win by doing fewer things better—and making those things easy to repeat.

As you think about your own systems, remember: clarity and simplicity don't limit growth; they fuel it.

WHY SYSTEMS?

1. A *system* is a group of technology, processes, functions, and people that work together to achieve a goal, while org structure is a continual process and is the starting point for systems to work properly.
2. Systems will help you grow and develop as a company, but most systems will not be successful without Healthy Leaders. Your leaders will be the reasons for good integration and results.
3. Good systems allow for delegation and empowering your employees.

CAUTION

1. Never form systems without diagnosing first. You want to invite others into forming a way together.
2. Integration is the hardest phase of system creation. Ensure you plan well and never promise perfection.
3. Even one leader who doesn't embrace empowering others through systems can hinder the rest of your company.

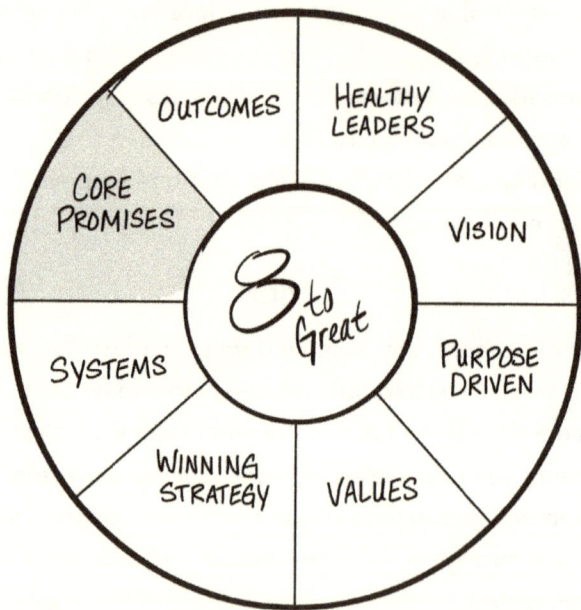

SEVEN

ALIGNING WITH CORE PROMISES

99% ARE MISSING THIS 1 THING

Kindness is a language which the deaf
can hear and the blind can see.

—MARK TWAIN

A FEW YEARS AGO, I had a firsthand encounter with what happens when a business lacks Core Promises, and it all unfolded at a fast-food restaurant. As we pulled in, my wife and I noticed something rare: an empty drive-thru. *Jackpot!* We quickly placed our order and pulled up to the window, expecting a smooth and speedy experience. Instead, we encountered chaos.

Inside, we heard through the closed window employees shouting across the kitchen. Suddenly, the window slid open. An employee, barely engaged, blurted out, "Did you order the hamburgers and kid's meals?" My wife politely confirmed, and with zero explanation, the employee simply replied, "Great!" took our payment, and told us to pull forward. The problem? The only thing in front of us was the exit. So, we inched forward just enough to make room for the next car, assuming our food would be right behind us. Ten minutes passed. Then, 15.

By the 20-minute mark, I started thinking I've had faster service at the DMV. No updates, no apologies—just waiting. It was a perfect example of a business running without a clear standard of excellence, without promises to their customers, and without anything that made them memorable—for the right reasons. Unfortunately, we've all been there as businesses.

Now, compare that to one of many experiences we've had at Chick-fil-A. The drive-thru line was overflowing into neighboring parking lots, and at first, we thought, *This is going to take forever*. But then we reminded ourselves—*they've mastered this*. So, we pulled in, knowing we were locked into the line.

Within 5 minutes, we reached the ordering section, where 3 well-dressed employees in hi-viz vests were outside, taking orders with a smile. A young worker greeted us warmly, took our order with enthusiasm, and sent us on our way. As we moved forward, my wife said, "Thank you," and, without hesitation, they each responded, "My pleasure."

Moments later, our hot food was handed to us, and we drove off. We couldn't help but talk about how seamless the experience was—how they always say "my pleasure" and how their team is consistently polite, well-trained, and laser-focused on keeping things moving. It's no accident. They're built on intentional service and unwavering standards. Their Core Promises are clear.

Let's unpack how to create clear, meaningful promises that differentiate your brand and drive loyalty.

CORE PROMISES:
THE STUFF YOU ACTUALLY DELIVER

So, what are Core Promises? They are the most definitive within all the Operational 4 components of the 8 to Great. They are the *positive absolutes* that no matter what, customers and employees expect and know you for. They are built on brand promises but become distinct in how they are measured and clear to all your customers. Core Promises shape your reputation and create a sense of reliability that people associate with your business. There are 2 roads you can travel down in your business: compete on price or differentiation. This chapter is about how to be unique and add value that helps establish loyal customers time and time again.

Ultimately, Core Promises establish a sense of certainty and dependability. They build loyalty by ensuring that no matter the circumstances, people—both customers and employees—know exactly what they can expect from you. In this chapter, we will explore what makes Core Promises different from guarantees, sale promotions, taglines, and other brand promises. I'll show why they are so important and why they are a part of thriving businesses that last and how you can be known for something great no matter the size of your business. You'll learn how to create, revamp, and strengthen your promises into tangible, well-known expectations that add tremendous value to your customers and people.

THE MOMENT THEY DECIDE TO COME BACK

Consider your expectations when your HVAC system is being serviced. Is there a signature experience you can count on? Do they greet you a certain way, offer a unique touch, or go the extra mile with thoughtful details? For example, they may wear shoe covers, no questions asked or provide clear pricing on paper before any work begins.

Core Promises are the defining elements that set businesses apart, regardless of industry. They create consistency, build trust, and give customers reliable, positive experiences. Without them, you blend into the sea of competitors, reduced to just another option in a price-driven decision. Without them, there's no loyalty, no lasting impression, just another forgettable transaction. While no single Operational 4 element outranks the others, it's often a company's Core Promises that leave the biggest impact. If done right, they're what people remember most about doing business with you.

We believe there are many businesses that have good Core Promises. It takes some examples to see the relevance of how powerful they are. In the Purpose Driven chapter, we discussed how purpose drives so many things in your business. Purpose can and will often be directly tied to your Core Promises. Check out some examples. Each of these companies below has a stated Core Promise with clear purpose.

- **Patagonia** is committed to environmental sustainability and social responsibility, including using recycled materials, repairing used gear, and pledging 1% of sales to environmental causes. Their employees and customers can depend on them to give back to helping the environment. The 1% is clear and measurable.

- **L.L.Bean:** If you're not 100% satisfied with 1 of their products purchased directly from L.L.Bean's website, stores, or catalog, you may return it within 1 year of purchase for a refund. This is a Core Promise that flows from their purpose, "We believe the more time you spend outside together, the better. That's why we design products that make it easier to take longer walks, have deeper talks and never worry about the weather. It's like our Founder always said—being outside brings out the best in us."

• **FedEx** is known for "Absolutely, positively overnight." This is clear that they are dependable for overnight shipping. This timeline is simple and measured as a promise: did you make it happen or not? Customers will trust them when they deliver on their Core Promise.

These companies have identified their purpose and given clear Core Promises that we know and love when buying from them. That's why we believe that Core Promises is a component of thriving businesses. It truly separates them from others and helps create loyalty, not bottom dollar buyers. You could be wondering what the difference is between other promises, guarantees, and Core Promises. They can be similar, but we believe that Core Promises are clearly different because they are concrete expectations and behavior that customers depend on and you become known for.

Core Promises should be more rigid in how they're communicated and leave no room for error of interpretation. There's no hidden *terms and conditions*. No room for error is simple like saying "my pleasure" when interacting with every customer. Also, Core Promises are not a sale, seasonal guarantee, or a one-off. They reveal a journey of commitment that your customers and employees come to expect. This is a component of the 8 to Great because humans want consistency, but most of us lack it. Great businesses will fight to be consistent. They will strive to show employees and customers that they are the most dependable and memorable in their industry.

Promises Only Work If You Can Prove Them

To eliminate any lingering confusion, let's break this down with an example—no names, no judgment. Imagine you own a gym with the purpose of providing a clean, well-equipped, and affordable space for the average joe. That's a noble purpose. But let's be honest—just *saying* you're a clean gym isn't enough. You can't slap, "We're clean!" on a billboard and expect people to believe it without something to back it up. Though it might be a part of your brand promise, you need a measurable Core Promise that keeps you accountable and earns trust. For example, if cleanliness is your thing (and in the gym world, it better be), you could make a Core Promise like this: "Our staff performs cleanliness checks and touch-ups every hour." Now your customers know exactly what to expect, and you've got something that holds you accountable. Employees now have clear direction and know how to uphold your promise. It's not just a vague feel-good statement—it's a concrete, measurable promise that connects directly to your purpose of providing a clean gym. Plus, it's a lot easier to promote "Hourly checks" than trying to convince people you're clean just because you *said so*. To make this even more clear, you might build a system that requires employees to write their initials next to that handy checklist and instructions posted on the wall for all customers to see. This is a clear example of how Core Promises don't need to cost a ton of money to provide huge value to customers.

The measurable is where many businesses fall short. We love catchy phrases like "quality, speed, and accuracy," but unless there's a Core Promise tied to those claims, it can be empty fluff. Customers are savvy. They're not impressed by vague aspirations; they want proof. It's like Chick-fil-A's famous "My pleasure." Sure, it's a simple phrase, but it's a powerful promise. Every time you hear it, you know the team is trained to deliver a certain level of service, and if they don't say it, you'll notice.

DON'T JUST BE CATCHY; BE VALUABLE

It might be tempting to ask after reading this, "What is our Core Promise?" But before you ask that, it's more important to ask the question, "What can I promise that will bring the highest value to customers?"

Core Promises are not just something you want to get recognized. If that was the case, we would all just come up with catchy gifts that are dished out for everyone. Surely, people would know and talk about your company more if you left them fortune cookies. People might at first think, *Okay, I love fortune cookies*. But after a bit, they are going to wonder how it correlates with your business. If you're a Chinese restaurant, you're doing pretty good, as expected, but every other business may have a hard time connecting the dots. Even though it might get some talk around town. If it doesn't add value, it's most likely not going to create customer loyalty. We've even heard of companies implementing, "My pleasure," copying the originator. Now, that might sound like a good idea, but the problem is that it's not genuine to their business, and often, it's not true to their culture. "My pleasure" is directly tied to Chick-fil-A's purpose: "To glorify God by being a faithful steward of all that is entrusted to us. To have a positive influence on all who come in contact with Chick-fil-A."

You can't steal that, thinking it will work for you too.

You also might have multiple Core Promises, each one will resonate differently with customers, but as long as it brings high value to them, they will see it as a genuine approach. In essence, each Core Promise will either move customers toward your offering (service or product), or away. This, of course, is dependent on the customer's needs and wants. Some Core Promises might fall outside the *circle* of your offering (see sketch). You'll want to realign those promises to ensure they bring value to your customers.

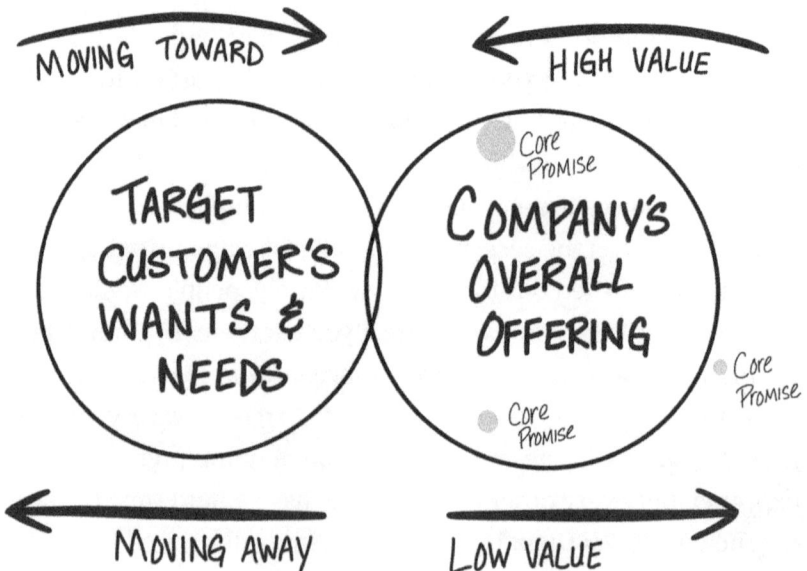

MOVING TOWARD   HIGH VALUE

TARGET CUSTOMER'S WANTS & NEEDS

COMPANY'S OVERALL OFFERING

Core Promise

Core Promise

Core Promise

MOVING AWAY   LOW VALUE

Here's a good example: a supply company has a Core Promise of "A real person and employee will always answer the phone to help." This is a Core Promise that not only attracts customers who desire that, but it also keeps the company accountable not to use automated software or a person in another country to answer their phones. They might also have a Core Promise that "All deliveries are 100% on time or it's on us." Both of these Core Promises bring high value and move the customer toward their product.

BRIDGE THE GAP BETWEEN EXPECTATION AND REALITY

Having the best Core Promises is also about understanding how you find ways to close the gap between expectations and reality. Expectations are what we have going into any situation. For example, the weather outside showing a sunny forecast. We expect that we will have a good day to do outside activities like a company cook-out. Reality is what will actually happen, like the weather showing a sunny forecast, but then pouring rain, rudely interrupting your company cookout.

This applies to internal and external people of your business. For instance, if your sales team is out there giving away the world, meanwhile the design and operations team is left to pick up the pieces, you'll have trouble having any Core Promise that add value to customers. You can't have major dysfunction and expect Core Promises to help enhance your service and product. Strengthening the connection of expectations and reality is a must to provide any viable promise.

You might be wondering why reality and expectations are the focal point. Think about any relationship. How about marriage for instance? How is it possible that 2 humans in a long-term committed relationship can often be on different planets when communicating? Picture this, your spouse tells you it would be nice to have a service that picked up groceries and brought them to your house. You know this already exists, but you just chime in and say, "Yeah, that would be cool." I think you probably know who's who in this scenario, but the spouse that relays this random dream, most likely, isn't being random at all. Maybe they're wanting you to discuss using a service that brings the groceries to the house. Or maybe they're thinking how it would be nice for you to ask for the list, go get the groceries, and bring them home in one fell swoop. If you've watched comedian Nate Bargatze, you probably just chuckled. Type his name into a browser and "one fell swoop" and enjoy. Back to the point, we often say or do things that feel like we're being forthcoming and transparent, but the other human doesn't pick it up the way we're laying it down.

That's because human relationships are super hard, and we often have a gap between our expectations and the reality that exists, especially when it comes to communication. This same kind of scenario happens in business all the time. Whether it's our employees or customers, we all have our own perspectives, and oftentimes, we believe we are communicating effectively, but in reality, we are on 2 different pages. We call this the *gap*. In order to bridge the gap of reality and expectations, we need to ensure we're covering all the ground necessary so that we can add the value to our Core Promises.

REALITY & EXPECTATIONS—THE GAP

When it comes to building strong business relationships, we've all experienced the frustration of misaligned expectations. Whether it's a project that fell short of what was promised or a misunderstanding that led to disappointment, these *gaps* can damage trust and hinder success.

Core Promises exist to close that gap. But before we even get there, we have to address the 4 factors that open it up in the first place: Clarity, Direction, Transparency, and Communication.

You might have the best service or product in your industry, but if you don't communicate it well, or if the direction your team takes is muddy or misaligned, the customer's expectations will never fully match the experience you intended. The result? Disappointment, no matter how good your offering is.

That's why I want to be clear: this only works if you've already nailed down quality. If your product or service isn't solid, none of this can help you. But assuming you're delivering quality, aligning these 4 variables—Clarity, Direction, Transparency, and Communication—will bring your customer's expectations and your business's reality into alignment. That's the foundation Core Promises are built on. I'll also mention, there are other variables you could replace, but these 4 are a good starting point.

When expectations and reality fully overlap, your customers know what they're getting and trust that they'll get it every time. That kind of trust is what sets you apart as a truly valuable partner.

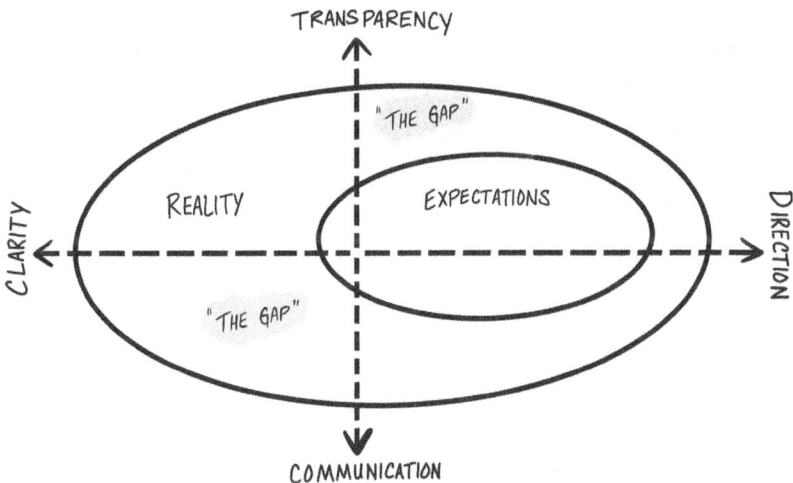

By evaluating how each variable interacts, you can identify where breakdowns occur and take actionable steps to improve. For example, if communication is strong but transparency is lacking, you might find customers still feeling lost despite regular updates. The key is not just to focus on one area but to create balance and consistency across all 4 variables. Establishing Core Promises isn't just about avoiding pitfalls. It's also about building a reputation for reliability and trustworthiness. When your customers know they can count on you to meet or exceed expectations every time, you create lasting loyalty and a strong foundation for growth.

Transparency

Transparency is about helping customers see you are trustworthy in how you operate. But it's not about sharing every detail to the detriment of the relationship. *What you see is what you get* is often a phrase that helps explain transparency. People should know that you are not trying to do something different than promised when no one is looking. Transparency can be as simple as itemizing a bill, recording hours on a project, sharing foreseeable obstacles when you find out about them, giving refunds or discussing compromises when you don't deliver best work, and the list goes on. Transparency is 1 part of how we can bridge the gap of reality and expectations to help form our best Core Promises. As stated before, we can have good transparency, or not, but when we don't, we will see expectations and reality become misaligned, creating frustration and poor Core Promises. Transparency paired with communication will build trust.

Transparency is specific to showing that you are trustworthy—what you see is what you get.

Communication: Double Tap

Transparency is tied directly to communication. Communication is a tool that we possess but often gets easily distorted in today's business world. Communication has so many channels like texts, emails, direct messages, calls, apps, and who knows what else...oh wait! I almost forgot—verbal and non-verbal, person-to-person communication. The better your communication channels and transparency, the more trust you will build with your relationships, including customers, and ultimately bridge the gap between their expectations and reality. Communicating well is essential and will always be valued for any business. Without excellent communication, Core Promises won't bring value to your customers.

Communication is specific to all applicable channels of good communication in your business.

One way to build habits to improve communication is what I call *double tap*. Double tap is when you use 2 forms of communication to ensure it's received accurately. For example, you have a meeting with your team and give direction on how to move forward with a difficult customer. To enhance this communication, a simple recap email is sent to participants to ensure accuracy. Here are simple, yet effective examples of how to *double tap*:

- After leaving a voicemail for a customer, follow up with a text.
- After a training session, send a personalized video with a quick recap of what was discussed, even showing a few tips you went over.
- Call a client the day before a meeting and ask if they had anything in particular to discuss beyond the agenda.
- For all meetings, ensure an agenda is sent out with clear timeframes and the goal of the meeting listed at the top.
- After agreeing on a deadline, send an invite with a clear day and time with an appropriate reminder.

- After a meeting, send the notes through a platform like MS Teams. List any actions and who is responsible for them.
- After sending a critical email, check in with each person by phone or face-to-face to hear their thoughts.

Clarity

Be crystal clear! Clarity is the never-ending pursuit of helping customers foresee obstacles and creating a clear path to agreed expectations. It can be as simple as ensuring there are scheduled meetings or times to review and create the clarity needed.

Let's continue to use an HVAC service company as an example. Imagine they show up to your house (wearing shoe covers) because your furnace shut off and it's in the middle of winter. First, to bring clarity, they go over the list of how they will diagnose the problem and move forward. They assure you that they will work diligently to understand the problem. They even show you their steps on an iPad or paper. This gives you confidence that there is a mutual understanding of expectations, which helps close the gap that may or may not exist. During the diagnosis, they take quick breaks to share their findings and next steps. Before they start to repair anything, they give you a plan for parts and labor and ask for your approval. Clarity is all about laying a path that is clear.

Clarity is specific to helping foresee outcomes and creating a clear path to agreed expectations.

Direction

This is specifically showing progress of getting to the end goal and is tied directly to clarity. For example, let's go back to the HVAC company that's been working on your furnace. They can be transparent, showing they are trustworthy. They can communicate extremely well through all the channels necessary. They can even provide huge amounts of clarity to align expectations. But if they can't give progress to the end goal of helping you fix your furnace, there is no Core Promise that will ever make a difference to you, the customer. Direction is about ensuring that progress is being made and relayed so that there is an agreed-upon path to the end goal. For instance, the HVAC company has a clear end goal of fixing the furnace. But maybe, it changes from fixing to installing a new one if the old one is not repairable. They will need to be transparent about the issue, communicate correctly, provide clarity on next steps, and give direction on how to proceed to accomplish the goal of getting heat to your house.

The expectations of the customer probably just changed right? They might have started out with the expectation of a repair, but now replacing it means more money. This means that you will have to double down on the 4 variables to help close the gap of expectations and reality. You might need to ensure you provide a specific schedule of how long it will take, plus show your breakdown of the cost, and any warranties that come with it. You might want to show them your financing options (hint-hint) or let them know that you provide competitive pricing and testimonials to ensure they know you're a good choice. No matter how many times direction changes due to circumstances, it's your job to reveal the direction to the goal, along with the other 3 variables, to close the gap.

Direction is specific to ensuring progress is being made toward the end goal.

Timely Speed

Timely speed is the driver that gives relevance to all 4 variables in the model. Imagine each dotted line on the model displaying the words, *speed* and *timeliness* (I would have added it, but the sketch just looked cluttered with it...just couldn't do it). Without timely speed being part of transparency, communication, clarity, and direction, your business might suffer even though you are executing on them. For example, transparency is useless, if it's not timely. People need and should receive transparency when it's applicable, not days or weeks later. When it's timely, people can act on it faster with more relevant information. The same goes for any of the other 3 variables. This seems like a lot to remember, but at the end of the day, thriving businesses are expanding in all these areas to ensure expectations and reality have little to no gaps. Only then can Core Promises be implemented with any real value to your customers.

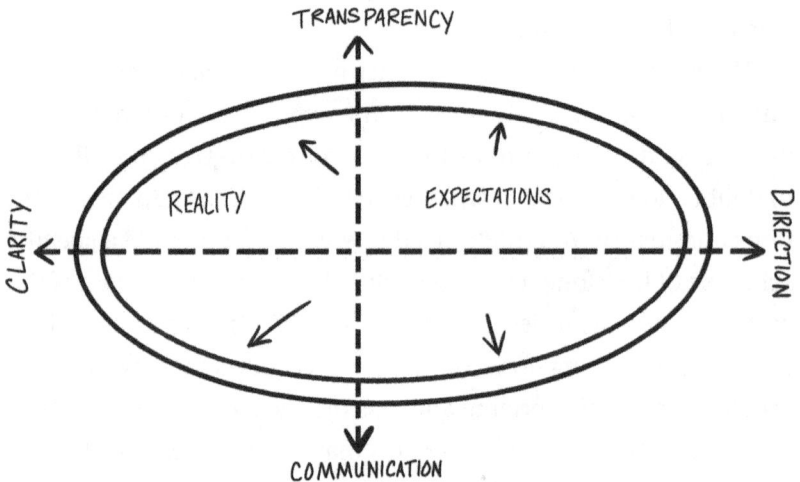

Build Alignment & Trust

When it comes to building strong Core Promises, the goal is not just to avoid missteps but to create a business that thrives on alignment and trust. When your operations are built on a foundation of Transparency, Communication, Clarity, and Direction—executed with timely speed—you transform potential gaps into seamless experiences. These elements work together to ensure your business consistently meets or exceeds customer expectations. The true power of Core Promises lies in their ability to create predictable, reliable outcomes for your customers. When every interaction is grounded in these principles, you build a reputation for excellence, cultivate lasting relationships, and pave the way for sustainable growth. By committing to these practices and regularly evaluating where gaps might appear, you take control of your business's narrative—one where expectations and reality are perfectly aligned.

DRIFT HAPPENS—JUST DON'T IGNORE IT

We all need to *close the gap* to create and maintain truly great Core Promises, but let's be honest—this isn't something that happens overnight. Developing Core Promises that genuinely add value to your customers is a process of trial, refinement, and consistency. It's the cumulative effect of repeatedly delivering on those promises that earns trust over time. Only when customers begin to rely on you, knowing with confidence that you'll follow through, do Core Promises solidify into a powerful foundation for your business. Of course, mistakes will happen. You will, inevitably, fall short of delivering on a Core Promise at some point. It might be a big misstep with your best customer or a seemingly minor moment, like an employee forgetting to say, "My pleasure." Big or small, these missteps matter, because every time you fail to deliver on a Core Promise, you risk eroding the trust that took so long to build.

Author Andy Stanley said, "We don't drift into good directions. We discipline and prioritize ourselves there." The goal isn't perfection but vigilance: acknowledging when you've gone off course and taking immediate action to correct it. Think of your business as a ship. A slight drift off course may not seem like a big deal at first, but over time, if unaddressed, that drift can take you far from the destination you've worked toward for years, or even decades. Every decision, every interaction, and every choice matters, because they collectively shape the promises your customers and employees come to depend on. Making mistakes isn't the real danger. The tragedy lies in failing to course-correct, allowing those Core Promises to weaken until they no longer hold weight. The good news? This is all within your control. By being intentional, responsive, and committed to the promises that define your business, you can build a reputation of unwavering reliability. It's a long game, but one worth playing. Every time you deliver on your promises, you're not just meeting expectations, you're reinforcing your company's DNA. Stay the course, correct the drift, *close the gap*, and let your Core Promises serve as the compass that leads to sustained success.

Writing this chapter was *my pleasure*...I hope that joke landed.

TAKE-IT-WITH-YOU NOTE

Core Promises are the most definitive among all the Operational 4 components. They are the positive absolutes *that no matter what, customers and employees expect and know you for. Core Promises shape your reputation and create a sense of reliability that people associate with your business.*

BONUS: CHICK-FIL-A'S PROMISES BEHIND THE COUNTER

While this chapter presents Core Promises primarily through a customer-facing lens, I believe there's an equally powerful (and often overlooked) dimension: the Core Promises we make to our employees. When leadership makes clear, intentional commitments to their team and follows through, it builds deep trust, loyalty, and alignment. In turn, employees are far more likely to deliver exceptional experiences to customers.

A standout example of this is Chick-fil-A. (I keep mentioning this company, because I love God's chicken.) Since 1946, they've upheld a now-famous Core Promise: closing all locations on Sundays. This decision, rooted in founder Truett Cathy's personal convictions, offers employees a guaranteed day of rest, reflection, or worship. This is especially rare in the demanding, fast-paced restaurant industry.

Of course, this promise hasn't come without challenges. Closing on one of the busiest days of the week requires operational discipline and unwavering commitment to purpose. And yet, Chick-fil-A has remained one of the most successful and admired fast-food chains in America. Their Sunday closure is more than a policy; it's a symbol of integrity. It's a Core Promise lived out consistently, year after year, across every location.

The beauty of it is that it's easily measurable. They either open on Sundays or they don't. Customers feel it too, especially when they pull into the drive-thru after church, only to be greeted by the unmistakable disappointment of locked doors. It stings, but it's also a reminder of their values, and a commitment that earns widespread respect.

When companies make and keep meaningful promises to their people, it creates a ripple effect. Employees show up more engaged, more empowered, and more motivated to serve others, proving that internal alignment drives external excellence through their Core Promises.

WHY CORE PROMISES?

1. Core Promises define what customers and employees can always expect and depend on, shaping your reputation and creating a sense of reliability that people associate with your company.

2. Purpose can and will often be directly tied to your Core Promises.
3. The Reality and Expectations Model is about *closing the gap* between what customers expect and what is reality. Ultimately, this creates trust and builds the best Core Promises.

CAUTION

1. Don't steal other company's Core Promises. It's unique to their culture and can't be replicated by imposters.
2. Don't create *bumper stickers*. Customers know if you're just using a catchy slogan or actually bringing value.
3. Core Promises take time to develop. Don't try to develop something overnight. Test and refine, add value to your customers, and become known for something. Ninety-nine percent won't do this well, but you can.

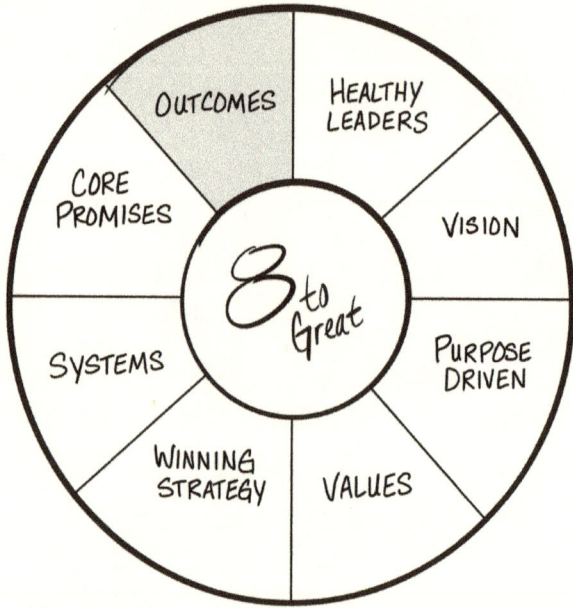

— EIGHT —

OUTCOMES CONTINUUM

Lead with Clarity, Measure What Matters

It is wiser to find out than suppose.
—MARK TWAIN

AVE YOU EVER QUESTIONED whether your business is truly performing at its best? Have you worried about losing quality, efficiency, or money but struggle to identify the exact problem? We've all been there. We need to know the results and how to keep track. Whether that's processes, people, or our products, all facets of our companies need a results-driven culture.

Years ago, I was working with a small manufacturing company, and the employees welcomed me with open arms. I was pumped to be there, our values aligned, and I enjoyed the thought of working together. But before I received the partnership, in one of our initial meetings, the president came in and sat down. He was an older gentleman with an extremely humble demeanor but showed *poker face* authority. He asked, "How will I know that you can help us improve?" I've heard this question before of course. Normally I would say something like, "I can show you our process and client resume."

But I knew that wouldn't give him the confidence he needed. So, I answered a question with a question (timeless move), "How do you know your business is winning?" He said without hesitation, "We are generating more revenue year after year." "Great!" I said. I then asked, "How do you know you're getting better, not just adding more revenue?" He looked at me for a second, smiled, and said, "I don't. I guess that's why you're here."

Later, as we walked the floor, I stopped to ask multiple employees, "How many products have you produced this week?" Without much hesitation, multiple responses were, "No idea, am I supposed to know that?" They were making quality products every day, and no one could tell me how many they made that day, let alone that week. They were playing the game with no scoreboard. Even though they made high-quality products, they didn't know where they were winning.

This chapter is about measuring what matters, so you know what's working, what's not, and where to improve.

FROM NUMBERS TO MEANING

That story may or may not resonate with you, but think about how this applies to every company, no matter what you sell or industry you're in. W. Edwards Deming, recognized as the father of quality management, said, "In God we trust, all others bring data." Data is necessary to help you know if you're winning. Beyond your typical company data like revenue, net profit, cash flow, etc., businesses should know data on less talked about areas. For example, do your employees know what's getting done for the week or the month? Do they know how much rework has been required on jobs or how many products didn't pass inspection? Do they know what's complete or still pending? Do they understand how their work is contributing to the success of the company? If your answer is no, you are probably missing a key ingredient in your business—tracking and sharing. Sounds elementary, but Outcomes rest on the key components of tracking, accountability, and balanced with sharing information.

This chapter is different from just showing how data is important. Numbers and data are raw facts: things like sales figures, website traffic, or customer counts. They provide insight into *what* happened but don't necessarily explain *why* it happened or *what it means* for the business. Outcomes, on the other hand, goes deeper by measuring the impact of those numbers. In other words, data is like keeping score, while outcomes tell the story behind the score.

In this chapter, you will learn the power of understanding what true development is and how it's linked to tracking outcomes, not just *feeling* good about it. You'll learn the key areas that every business should pay attention to and give you insightful ways to do it. You'll walk away with practical applications for your individuals, teams, and company results.

YOU CAN'T JUST FIX. YOU HAVE TO CELEBRATE

If we only speak about all the things we can improve on in our businesses, people will get burnt out. Many businesses know this but can't help themselves to talk mostly about the things that need improvement. We need to be relentless about praising and correcting consistently. If you're a parent, you totally get this. Kids need praise and also discipline. Tracking outcomes is more than knowing what needs improved. It's also about knowing what to celebrate.

Share the Mistake, Skip the Blame

Each of us is hopefully learning lessons every day, little and big ones, but rarely do we take the time to record them as a company. There are many software platforms that specialize in helping with this, like learning management systems, but this can be as simple as an online shared folder, where anyone can input a lesson learned. This becomes an important resource for training, course correcting, and building. When people within your company make mistakes, but others don't learn from the mistake, then you're missing out on development. Obviously, this is not about calling out names or having someone come to the middle of the room while you share their faults. This is more of a discreet broad sharing to help others learn faster. We have helped implement this very thing in many companies, but one in particular I remember because the president took it so seriously. When they would have their leadership meetings, someone would inevitably talk about a mistake made, and as soon as it came out of their mouth, the president would say, "Did you put that in our database?" It became part of their culture to learn fast from their mistakes.

It's important that you create a culture where people know their names aren't going to be called out, but their *lessons* will be.

When leaders are *inconsistent* in lessons learned, I see problems arise. Meaning, one day, they let something slip, then the next, they are cracking down on it. Inconsistency in this will lead to problems. This creates fear among your employees. People can feel pointed out as failures,

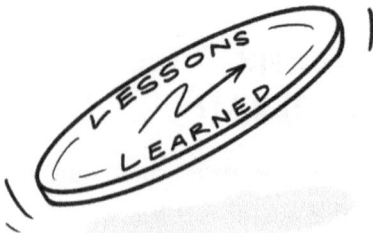

but when companies have *consistency* in lesson sharing, I see a culture that embraces their mistakes and learns faster.

Celebrate What You Want Repeated

This is my favorite, mainly because it drives Personal and Collective Purpose. When we do a good job of celebrating the small and big wins of our teams, we replicate those results. If you have kids, you know this to be true: what we praise has a better opportunity for repeating. And guess what? We're all grown-up kids.

I've worked with many companies who have done this well. DANCER, a prior mentioned business, has a weekly personalized email from the president to his employees. The beginning of it always starts with a quote from a customer about one of their projects. That same email ends with praising each individual team for their progress. Another company we've encountered has included services to the customer like construction project drone videos. Those same employees have access to the videos to see the wins for each project. They have created a way to show how their employees work is connected to the final result. When you can connect an employee's job to the product or service, people get to see the end result and ultimately, have more buy-in. That is the power of celebrating wins. You connect their purpose to the collective whole and feel united. Wins celebrated is about helping praise what should be repeated in your business.

THE INFINITE LOOP

Outcomes is about understanding that your results are an infinite loop, not a one and done or a periodic check-in. Thriving businesses track results consistently. Peter Drucker, famously titled the father of management, said, "What gets measured gets improved." I created the Infinite Loop sketch to give a structure for key areas to measure. It doesn't matter how you track results—whether you like KPIs, scorecards, or review meetings, outcomes should be tracked and understood by your leaders and their teams. Keep in mind though, when I say outcomes, I mean you are tracking results, not just tasks that get done. The point is to move toward increased value to your employees and customers, so checked-off tasks will not, alone, be sufficient to know if you are getting true results. Each category of the Infinite Loop reveals the *pockets* of your business that you track for results: Healthy Leadership, Winning Strategy, Team Outcomes, Employee Outcomes, Customer Outcomes, and Org Outcomes. These are woven together with goals and feedback.

Healthy Leadership: Behavior Tracked

In Chapter 1, we discussed what Healthy Leadership means, so we won't be redundant. For the purposes of Outcomes, think about this: when your leaders treat your people like they matter the most, your teams will flourish, and your customers will feel it too. Far too often we see companies scrambling to do anything for their customers at the expense of their employees, maybe you've even done this in your business. It's not without good intention, right? Your customers are the ones who pay the bills—shouldn't employees do anything for them? Not if you want to be a thriving, self-sustaining business. For years, we've seen companies drain their employees, and for many, this meant high turnover and paying more money to keep top talent. It's a vicious cycle that we might think is necessary, but in reality, we can end the cycle with a better outlook and culture.

A while back, I worked with a team who couldn't get out of the limelight, and as a result, customers kept coming. They were a larger company, where many of the leaders almost felt trapped, and they needed to keep servicing clients who had been with them for decades. When we started to work with their team, we realized through our diagnosis that employees felt this burden, and it was starting to take a toll. Their turnover rate was high, yet they were applying for awards like "Best Company to Work For." The leadership team finally realized that their awards had little worth when employees kept leaving. On the exit interviews, there were many recorded statements like, "Employees took a backseat to customer demands."

The Infinite Loop starts with Healthy Leadership. Leaders who truly care about developing their people and themselves through the GIG: Growing, Investing, and Guiding. Here are questions to track with your leaders. Though a bit more subjective, these questions are aimed towards behavior, not just numerical results.

- Are they learning, or just busy? What intentional growth or development have they pursued lately, or are they just treading water?
- Can they lead when you're not in the room? Are they empowering their team, making decisions, and owning outcomes—or waiting for direction?
- Is their team growing or just surviving? Are people under their leadership getting better, clearer, and more aligned—or silently burning out?

- Do they know what success looks like each day? Are their responsibilities tied to measurable outcomes, or are they drowning in a to-do list with no scoreboard?
- Would your customers rave about their impact? Do they create a ripple effect that makes the customer experience better, or are they part of the friction?
- Are they owning the numbers or dodging them? When results are offtrack, are they the first to face it, fix it, and rally the team—or point fingers and pivot topics?
- Are they playing to win or just playing not to lose? Are they setting bold goals, inspiring action, and moving the needle— or just maintaining the status quo?

Most businesses we work with will not have trouble tracking number-based outcomes. They struggle to hold leaders accountable to their behavior and the company values.

Winning Strategy: Tracking Toward Vision

Congruent with Healthy Leadership, we need to connect the dots to the Winning Strategy. Your leaders must be good at disseminating goals to their teams in order to be aligned across the business, ultimately helping drive toward your vision. These goals will help establish outcomes for your teams and individuals. Objectives from your Winning Strategy will be distributed to each department. Cascading your Winning Strategy to your teams is needed if you want to see movement toward your vision. Here are 2 questions that will help form results to track:

1. What goals need to hit the bullseye now, not later? Review your Winning Strategy objectives and review short-term deadlines.
2. Who has the bandwidth and horsepower to take on more? Review individuals who can handle extra work.

If we hit snooze on this for 6 months, what breaks? Predict and review the consequences you might have to live with if you pushed items on your strategy.

Team Outcomes: Collective Winning

Team Outcomes is about performance. You want to know if your teams are winning. Each team should have key daily, monthly, and periodic outcomes that are tracked to ensure your business is aligned and moving in the right direction. An example could be as simple as project hand-off meetings. You could track things like, how many hand-off meetings do they perform and how clear are expectations when they give the project to the next department? Tracking these outcomes will give indication of their performance. Team Outcomes is about a collective result. We should understand how well our teams can work together. Here are 3 questions to help create and track team outcomes. Put these in writing, plaster them to a hallway wall, door, put in a shared folder, on your software dashboard, etc. Do whatever it takes to ensure the team knows these:

1. What are the key outcomes that this team needs accountability on? You can put these in daily, weekly, or monthly results.
2. What are the key team results that will help the company know if we're winning? Much like the first question, but this one is more about how people will know if you're winning, not what you need accountability on.
3. What results are easy to forget about, but often need attention to stay on course? These are good to have in writing. All of our teams have things that we forget, but need to stay on top of mind. A quick example of this might be team development.

Employee Outcomes: Personal Development

These outcomes are more granular and individual. You should know if your chain (team) has a weak or strong link. Employees should expect that you're building a thriving culture that truly pays attention to results. This is not at the expense of caring for people but used as a way to measure progress and development.

Employee Outcomes should be separated in 2 parts: strategic and job responsibilities. Strategic results will derive from the objectives of your Winning Strategy. Those will then be made into individual goals if applicable.

EMPLOYEE
OUTCOMES

STRATEGIC   JOB

Their job responsibilities are the other key area. In order to be clear about job responsibilities, we suggest creating role cards. Role card reviews can be as often as needed, but I would suggest a reoccurring calendar invite so it is consistent and effective.

Below is an example of an actual employee role card. This card is a simple way to have accountability around clear expectations per your employee's responsibilities. It allows the leader and employee to have discussions around the results that are expected per the position. When the employee isn't fulfilling their responsibilities/outcomes, written plans to help steer them in the right direction should be developed. Put these notes on a shared drive to provide clarity. This is a form of double tap!

OUTCOMES CONTINUUM

OPEN/LOCKING UP	PREPARATION IS KEY	Open/Lock up the production floor, following all procedures, so that is ready for use next shift.
OVEN OPERATING	KEEP PRODUCTION FLOWING	Fill in any open oven operating space when needed and keep the team progressing when full.
COMMUNICATION	KEEP THE TEAM ON TRACK	Check in with each operator [#] times per shift. Give directions and training as needed.
TNR	THINK ONE STEP AHEAD	Work with operators to have tanks on deck for ovens. Check specs before sign-off for oven.
PRESENCE	BE THE EXPERT	Be available for all questions/emergencies. Clocked in and on the floor [time or marker].
DOCUMENTATION	MAINTAIN ACCURATE DATA	Keep the management team and prep team informed. Update [picking tickets?] [frequency].

Beyond results you are tracking for each employee, you can also create goals. This will balance results tracking with performance stretching. This allows you to hold them accountable for their job responsibilities and integrate goals from your Winning Strategy or to develop them in their daily responsibilities. Goal time frames should be set with clear deadlines. This could be a month, year, or whatever it takes for the desired outcome. An example could be to learn a new skill or shore up an existing one, or maybe it's to mentor a new employee. Just ensure it's clear how often leaders should meet with their employees to review and calibrate. All goals should be in writing and shared with team members consistently. Use our CALL list to help create as much clarity as possible for goal setting. Using these questions will help you ensure they are connected to the overall company direction.

- **C**larity of goals: list goals with clear expectations and desired outcomes.
- **A**ligned with the vision: what are some ways it will align and help move us to our vision?
- **L**ength of time: list the dates that matter the most: When the goals start, when you've reached big milestones, and when you expect to finish.
- **L**asting impact: list some ways the goals will have lasting impact for the employee and the company.

Customer Outcomes: Do They Brag About You?

While the customer's experience is vital, it's important to understand that it comes as a result of fostering Healthy Leaders and a strong internal culture. The sequence of results matters. When you treat your people like they truly matter, that care and attention naturally extend outward to your customers. It's a ripple effect: a team that feels valued and empowered will create exceptional experiences for the people they serve. However, tracking customer outcomes is critical to ensure that this alignment is happening and to make the necessary adjustments when it's not.

To gain a clear understanding of your customer experience, we recommend asking targeted, meaningful questions that give you actionable insights. This starts with using a simple 1–4 rating scale. Why not 1-0? Because the broader the scale, the more likely you are to receive middle-of-the-road answers that offer no clarity. A 1-to-4 scale forces customers to make a clear choice and lean one way or the other, providing you with a better sense of their true sentiments.

Here are 5 key questions that can help you track customer outcomes:

1. Overall, how satisfied are you with your experience with us?
2. How would you rate our interactions and communication with you?
3. How effectively did our team resolve any issues that came up?
4. How consistent were we from start to finish?
5. Overall, what value did we bring to you the most?

Don't just stop at the ratings. Encourage your customers to share their experiences through testimonials. These not only validate your efforts but also serve as powerful social proof to attract future customers. Be proactive about requesting quoted feedback. Specific, direct statements from your customers are far more impactful than vague praise.

Outcomes isn't just about celebrating the positive feedback. It's about embracing the negative as well. Continued growth comes from listening to the constructive criticism that customers share. Their honesty gives you the blueprint for improvement and development. When customers feel safe enough to be transparent, they're giving you a gift, which is the opportunity to address weaknesses, course-correct, and elevate your business.

Feedback Line: Know Faster

The Feedback Line from the sketch represents the mechanism that creates communication and understanding of true progress for results. Feedback Lines are essentially how you receive your results. They're how you know you're winning. An example of a Feedback Line is project dashboards from your operating software. This information might provide how many jobs are waiting for rework or which jobs are ready to start. Another example might be companywide surveys. Maybe you use something like Survey

Monkey. For many companies, this means department and leadership meetings, reports (hopefully automated), and product quality control. This requires people to input the right information to get the right feedback. Other great Feedback Lines are 360 reviews. There are many ways to get feedback from your team, but a typed email can work fine. There are also communication platforms like Microsoft Teams for transparent discussions between leaders and employees. It doesn't matter how small or big you are. Feedback Lines are important at any size.

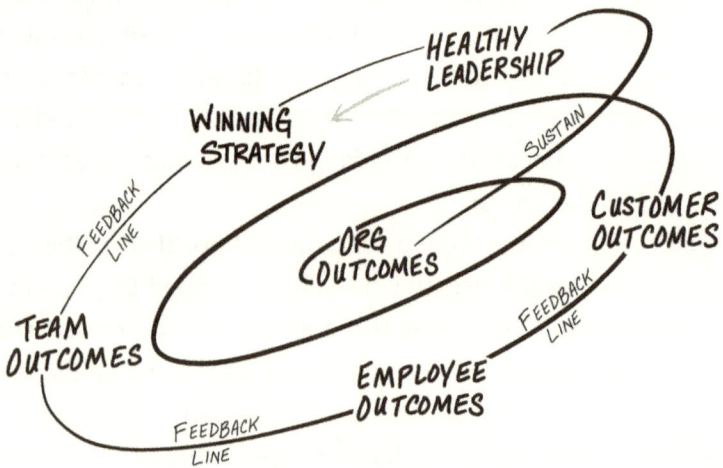

The challenge? Putting it all together so you don't have too many siloed areas where you receive the feedback. This could be as simple as exporting files to a spreadsheet with multiple tabs, an operating software like Monday.com, or Microsoft Teams with multiple channels. There are hundreds of options. Finding a place where your feedback can live in a few places versus many is a challenge, but achievable with research and clear guidelines. Without Feedback Lines being cohesive and brought together for holistic data, the risk is having a multitude of good information that no one sees or uses.

Org Outcomes: A Broad View

This is the last part before the Infinite Loop returns back to itself, to Healthy Leadership. Remember, it's a continuum, not a binary— one and done. They are all connected. Org Outcomes are about high-level tracking. Though we won't go in depth on these areas of Org Outcomes, here are some main areas to track:

- **Objectives tied to the Winning Strategy**: Track the progress at least quarterly.
- **Financial health**: Including gross revenue, net profit, and cash flow.
- **Revenue per employee**: This helps indicate whether growing revenue and employees continue to be balanced.
- **Employees attrition rate per department and company**: Tracking who is voluntarily leaving is a starting point to see how well you are retaining employees.
- **Employee satisfaction**: Use baseline questions to see progress each year.
- **Customer satisfaction**: Again, you can use surveys or just call them. I would track this quarterly at a minimum.
- **Customer referrals**: Always ask for referrals, even when you have too much work. This just might help you eventually be able to *fire* customers one day who don't align with your values and vision. You know what I'm talking about.

Tracking how many referrals you get gives you a good indication of how well you're doing with quality and timeliness.

Sustain: Never-Ending Loop

The Infinite Loop consistently and continuously tracks results. All starting points for outcomes are your leaders, ensuring they are embracing results and driving success. After that, all results are tied together and are equally important.

There are more outcomes to track depending on your industry and niche like website traffic, customer acquisitions cost, etc., but the ones above are a great start. Knowing these outcomes will help gauge which areas to build on and to shore up. One thing to remember is that these are indicators, but they don't necessarily relay root problems. Diagnose by going back to all the areas of the Infinite Loop.

YOU SHALL REMEMBER: D = L (A) P

Outcomes Continuum requires development. We all need to know our strengths in order to build on them and also, know our development opportunities in order to shore them up. At the end of the day, it's all about development. The more you develop as a company, the more you win. Development can be broken down as D = L (A) P.

DEVELOPMENT =

LEARNING X

(APPLICATION + ASSESSMENT)

X PERSISTENCE

Development: The Engine of Business Growth

Development isn't just a buzzword—it's the measure of whether we're improving, adapting, and ultimately succeeding. We all want to know if we're getting better, and knowing Outcomes demands that we not only track our progress but also actively develop in the areas we're measuring. Without intentional growth, we risk stagnation, falling behind competitors, and losing sight of our long-term vision. Development is how our companies will grow and have long-term success.

Learning: The Starting Point, Not the Destination

Development starts with learning, but too often, that's where it stops. How many times have you read an insightful book, attended a seminar, or watched an inspiring video, only to leave with a notebook full of ideas that never turn into action? Learning is essential, but knowledge alone doesn't create change. Without application and assessment, learning is just passive information gathering.

Application + Assessment: The Bridge to Real Growth

Applying what you learn is where true development happens. It's in the moments when we integrate knowledge into our businesses, test new strategies, refine habits, and push toward better results. But application without assessment is just blind action. We need to measure how well our efforts are working, course-correct when necessary, and ensure we're maximizing results. Application and assessment go hand in hand—one without the other leads to wasted effort or missed opportunities.

Persistence: The Key to Long-Term Success

If there's 1 factor that separates businesses that thrive from those that strive, it's persistence. The ability to keep moving forward despite obstacles, setbacks, or slow progress is what defines lasting success. Determination and consistency turn small efforts into big results over time. Think about the people in your life who have achieved something great. Chances are, they didn't stop when things got tough. Most people struggle with persistence, but those who develop it as a habit unlock the compounding effects of lifelong growth.

When we multiply learning by application and assessment, and then multiply that by persistence, development becomes inevitable. This is the formula for real, sustainable business growth.

The Power of D = L (A) P

Development isn't a 1-time event. It's a continuous journey that drives long-term success. The Outcomes reminds us that the process of improvement isn't just about celebrating wins—it's about embracing the lessons that come from setbacks, learning from them, and using them as fuel to get better. The equation $D = L\,(A)\,P$ serves as a framework for intentional, ongoing growth in your business and your life. It shows us that learning is just the beginning, application and assessment ensure meaningful progress, and persistence is the engine that keeps us moving forward, no matter the obstacles.

For your business to thrive, every part of this equation must be at work. Are you committed to learning new strategies and insights? Are you applying them thoughtfully and assessing their impact? Most importantly, are you pushing through challenges with persistence? We can't just hope for success. We must intentionally develop, learn, apply, assess, and persist.

This formula is a reminder that growth is a compounding process. Every step you take builds on the last, and over time, the results become exponential.

TAKE-IT-WITH-YOU NOTE

Outcomes are not just about the good results. It's just as important to understand the bad ones. We all need to know our strengths in order to build on them and also, know our development opportunities in order to learn and shore them up.

BONUS: KANSAS CITY CHIEFS IN THE BOARDROOM

I was sitting next to my friend and client, Tony Tranquill, president of Wayne Pipe and Supply. His son, Drue Tranquill, plays for the Kansas City Chiefs, the Super Bowl LVIII champions of 2023. The next year, they fought their way back to the 2024 Super Bowl with the same grit and tenacity, determined to bring home another big win. But this time, things didn't go their way. They had an off game and ended up losing to the Philadelphia Eagles. Most people might shrug it off and say, "Hey, they won last year—what's the big deal?" But Tony shared something that stuck with me. As he consoled his son Drue after the game, telling him how proud he was, Drue simply responded, "Nobody will remember who almost won the Super Bowl."

Let that sink in.

Getting to the Super Bowl is one thing, but getting to it again… now that's impressive in itself. But legacies aren't made on *good enough*. Now, imagine if we all had this mindset in our businesses. What if we realized that nobody remembers the company that *almost* made an impact? No one celebrates the business that was once on top but then crumbled like so many before them. What people remember—the companies that stand the test of time—are the ones that keep showing up, keep pushing forward, and keep making a difference.

The best teams, the best businesses, and the best leaders track progress relentlessly. They don't just celebrate past victories—they stay hungry, refining their strategy, adjusting their game plan, and pushing for the next win. In the end, nobody remembers who *almost* succeeded. They remember the ones who kept score, played to win, and never let up. I imagine we haven't seen the last of the Chiefs.

WHY OUTCOMES?

1. As a thriving company, you must track results/outcomes. This is a continuum, not a binary, 1-and-done type of tracking.
2. There are key areas that need tracked. This is known as the Infinite Loop. Each area is connected and always continues in the loop: Healthy Leadership, Team Outcomes, Employee Outcomes, Customer Outcomes, and Org Outcomes.
3. To track results well, you must be good at creating Feedback Lines that give you information fast. This helps you course-correct as needed and often as possible.

CAUTION

1. Don't get wrapped up in fancy words like KPIs and other methods that don't make sense for your culture. Ensure your people understand the key results for your business.
2. Don't overcomplicate it. The key is to understand that this is all leading to development. The more you develop as a company, the more opportunity you'll have.
3. Don't start and let it fade. As humans, we have a tendency to start something and let it slip away slowly until 1 day, you've lost more than you can count. Results-driven cultures are built on positive consistency.

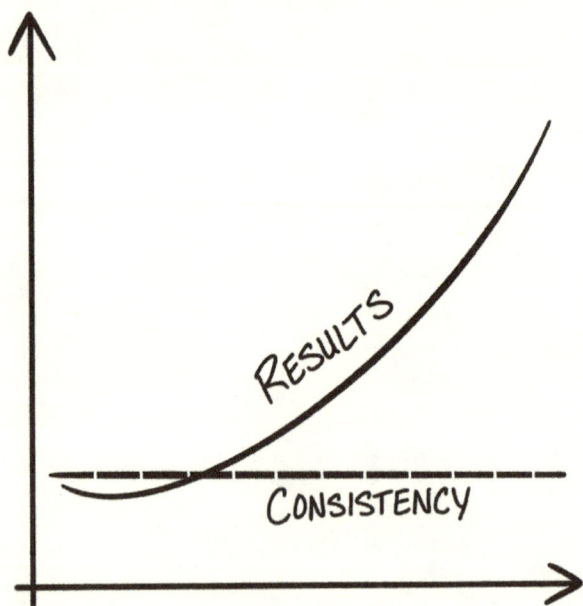

THE PATH TO THRIVING

To succeed in life, you need two things:
ignorance and confidence.
—MARK TWAIN

Okay, you made it to the end—congratulations! If I had to guess, you're probably less than 5% of the population. That means you have what it takes to continue on this narrow path of leading a thriving, self-sustaining business. This isn't rocket science; it's commitment. Commitment takes consistency, and results will compound over time for those who choose to go on the path.

You don't need a lifetime to build a self-sustaining business—one that runs without you but thrives with you. Freedom comes when you invest in people, lead with purpose, and streamline your operations.

I've seen businesses transform in a year, but most think this kind of business takes a lifetime. You now have the tools to get off that chaos roller coaster. You can create a business where you're in control *and* one that is purposeful. This kind of thriving business is no mystery. It's a framework of interconnected elements, each working in harmony to unlock extraordinary results.

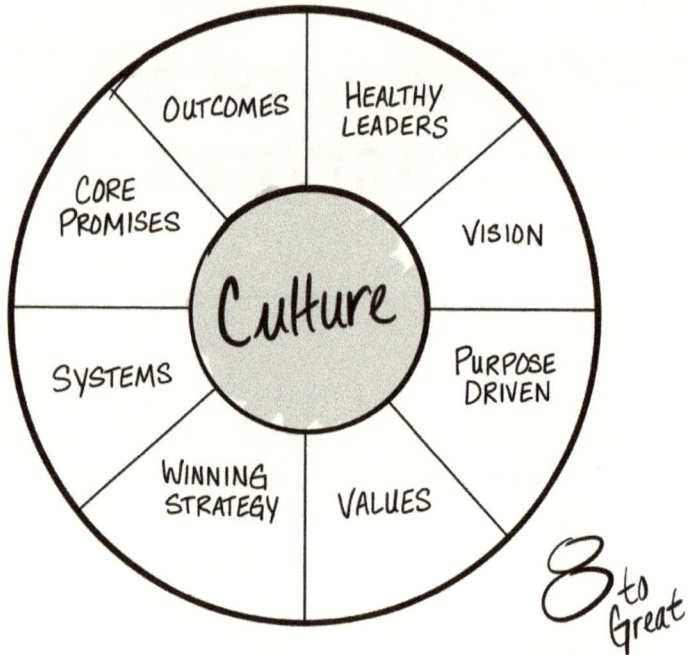

The 8 to Great is not just another business strategy—it's the blueprint for enduring success, built on principles that are as timeless as they are transformative. Imagine the potential of weaving this into the very fabric of your business. What could you achieve if your team operated with precision, purpose, and alignment at every level? The path requires unison, discipline, and persistence. It's the accountability measures to your culture and company. Much like anything worth pursuing in life, this kind of business does not just come to existence—you must work toward and care for it like any in-shape human body.

WHAT YOU WATER GROWS

Who's going to score this? Who will tell us when we're a thriving, self-sustaining company? Unlike many things in life, like certifications, there's no credits or auditors that will come and let you know. Thriving isn't a status. No one scores you, most won't even pay attention, and no one even has a clue until 1 day, people see the results of all your effort.

- They see that your leaders are people first. They take the GIG (Grow, Invest, Guide) seriously.
- They hear countless hours of you talking about vision. They see it guiding the company to new heights.
- Purpose has been integrated into everything you do. It invites others in and gives meaning.
- Values are driving beliefs, thoughts, and actions. They've become your decision filter and demand consistency.
- Your people start to see that strategy is not just a piece of paper—it's a way forward.
- They see that systems are in place, driving consistency and scalability.
- They know that they're expected to be consistent in their promises to the customer and that your customers see and feel the value.
- You hold others accountable for results because you want more for each other, not just profit.

All this is proven not in one moment, but with time and consistency. It moves you forward, proving that you're not just making it in the world; you're also paving the path for others. People will see that your business is a place where they want to work. Many will think they belong, but only those who choose to be on the same journey will profit from such hard work and dedication. Thriving is not a status. It is a choice every day to do what others will not.

Your Team Is Listening

The language you use matters. You need to channel your inner Yak Bak. Remember Yak Bak? Let me refresh your memory—it was this hilariously low-tech toy from back in the day. You'd record a quick 30-second snippet, and it would play it back to you, usually in a voice so warped and scratchy you'd wonder if it was possessed. But the magic of the Yak Bak was in its simplicity: you could repeat yourself, over and over, until the message (or whatever ridiculous noise you made) stuck.

As leaders, we need to take a page from the Yak Bak playbook. Repetition isn't annoying—it's essential. If you want your team to adopt the language, values, and mindset you're trying to build, you need to say it first. Then, say it again. And again. It's not enough to assume people just *get it* after one inspiring speech or a quick Slack message. Your beliefs, thoughts, and words are like seeds, and repetition is the water. Sure, much like the Yak Bak, the first attempts might come out a little fuzzy or choppy. Your grand vision might land more like "Eh, what?" That's okay. The key is to keep going. Clarity and impact come with time, patience, and practice.

When the communication inevitably goes sideways (because let's face it, it will), embrace your inner Yak Bak again. Just hit record and reframe, rephrase, and refine. You don't need to get it perfect every time. You just need to keep improving. Small wins in communication, whether it's a clearer explanation, a better metaphor, or even just remembering to repeat yourself in the first place will move you forward. It will all snowball into big successes over time. Language drives culture, and action follows language.

START SMALL. SHOW UP. STAY WITH IT.

Every company and leader has a unique way to position the 8 to Great, but there are some Do's and Don'ts that are helpful to hear:

- **Don't create an amazing grand plan and proposal before diving in**. Start with your leaders and involve them from day 1. Teach and discuss what it means to be a Healthy Leader. Grow with them, not one before the other.

- **Understand that you will not always get it right**. All good things take time. Ask for grace and be transparent that you don't have it all figured out. When we try to figure it all out before we start, we become trapped in a continuous thought of perfection, but have chosen to be in the cyclical state of sub-par.

- **Pay attention to people who are further in the journey than you are**. If we try doing it without paying attention to *the best*, we will miss a beautiful part of it all, community. One of the things I often hear leaders say is that they don't have a peer example who does what they do. But when they say *peer*, they often mean someone in their industry. They don't have to do exactly what you do to learn from them. Find others who are noticeably thriving and learn what you can.

- **Consistency only matters when done over time, not just for a period of time**. Put reminders on your calendar, schedule recurring meetings with your leaders, and plan and track progress. Intentionality and getting after it with some grit is good, but ensuring that you come back to it time-after-time will pay off. It's like *the art of showing up* when exercising. After a while, you will start to do more, be more, and see results.

Those results will become the force that pushes you to go further.

LET THEM BUILD THE HOW

One essential truth becomes clear: lasting success hinges on genuine engagement. Benjamin Franklin said, "Tell me and I forget. Teach me and I may remember. Involve me and I learn." We must learn to invite others to speak into the process and participate in meaningful ways. It's only when people feel heard and valued that they'll adopt what you, as a leader, know is needed. Engagement doesn't mean letting others dictate the direction. It's about creating a space where others' voices matter, where their ideas can shape the *how,* even as the *what* remains clear. The key lies in careful intentionality. Ask for input on what's still uncertain, where the *how* could benefit from fresh perspectives. The *what* is already defined, grounded in the *Foundational* and *Operational* components that guide you.

But the beauty of Healthy Leadership is recognizing that there's no universal blueprint. How you implement these components is unique to your team, your culture, and your company. Engagement is not a one-size-fits-all solution; it's a collaborative effort that grows from understanding, respect, and shared ownership. True engagement is not something you can force. You can't demand cohesion any more than you can demand someone to love you back. It's through actions like listening, involving, and leading with purpose that you earn respect and inspire others to adopt your vision as their own.

When done well, engagement transforms teams, strengthens culture, and ensures that everyone is fully aligned in pursuing something greater together. This is how you will thrive: not just by having the right components, but by bringing them to life through genuine collaboration.

FROM IDEAS TO ACTION

As you close this book, remember that the path to a thriving, self-sustaining business is a journey, not a destination. You've explored the essential components of the 8 to Great framework— from the Foundational to the Operational.

Now it's time to put these principles into practice. Take that first step forward. Review your business through the lens of 8 to Great. Identify your areas of biggest need and establish a regular cadence to work *on* your business with your leadership.

By investing in your people and processes, you'll unlock new levels of growth, profitability, and freedom. Your business will no longer depend on you, but it will empower you to do your best work.

The journey begins now. Embrace the challenge, trust the process, and watch as your company transforms from the inside out. The future is yours to create.

Let's get to work.

ACKNOWLEDGEMENTS

A project like this doesn't happen without support, feedback, and behind-the-scenes help.

Holly DeVaux: Thank you for dedication to this book and Living Water. You bring clarity and precision to our work, and many leaders are better because of it.

Larry Weigand and the team: I'm forever grateful for the opportunity that you have given me over the years. You have always embraced my techniques and have helped form this book in many ways.

Nick Dancer: Thank you for the encouragement and creative spark over the years—iron sharpens iron. You are an amazing leader, and I'm grateful for our friendship.

Tony Tranquill: You are and continue to be a great friend. It is an honor to be a part of your leadership story.

Willis and Brandenberger Family: It is an honor to be a part of your story, and I'm extremely blessed to have friends like you.

Steve Doepker: Thank you for being one of my first customers when I was just starting out as a high school entrepreneur. Your mentorship and friendship have played a big role in shaping who I am today.

Thank you to Pete Garceau for a simple but impactful book cover. Your art is unique and inspiring.

Thanks to Charlie Hoehn, Donnel McLohon, Lisa Caskey, and the publishing team at Author.Inc for your help shaping and sharpening this book.

As Sylvester Stallone once said during a speech, "I am the sum total of everyone I've ever met." I, too, am thankful for each person who helped bring clarity, energy, and forward momentum to this project and our firm's work.

ABOUT THE AUTHOR

My journey to becoming a business growth expert didn't start in a corner office or with a silver spoon. It started in the trenches of a small business under *painfully* poor leadership. And let me tell you, nothing will teach you faster than watching what not to do in real time. I saw firsthand how unclear direction, inconsistent decision-making, and reactive chaos could stall growth and crush morale like a boot on a flower.

Later, I joined a large construction company, where I swapped the chaos for clarity and began putting real strategy into motion. I didn't just observe this time. I rolled up my sleeves and helped lead initiatives that drove results *through* leaders, not around them. Over the next decade, I had the privilege of helping on the journey of doubling their revenue. We didn't just grow for growth's sake, but instead built systems and developed leaders that made the growth stick.

Today, I'm the founder of Living Water, a firm committed to helping businesses grow without losing their soul. My clients haven't just increased revenue (though that's nice); they've gained something even more valuable: the freedom to work *on* the business, not *be* the business.

With a master's degree in organizational development and what I call a *"street PhD"* in business growth (earned through years of trial, error, and more tea than I care to admit), I solidified the 8 to Great framework: a practical, proven path for growth through both people *and* processes.

This book, *Exit Without Leaving*, distills those principles into a clear guide for building a self-sustaining business that thrives with you, and one day, without you. Because the ultimate win isn't just more revenue; it's a business that doesn't fall apart when you finally take that long-overdue vacation.

www.ingramcontent.com/pod-product-compliance
Lightning Source LLC
Chambersburg PA
CBHW030502210326
41597CB00013B/754